ORDINARY
HEROES

ORDINARY HEROES

A MEMOIR OF 9/11

JOSEPH PFEIFER

*First FDNY Chief at
the World Trade Center*

PORTFOLIO / PENGUIN

Portfolio / Penguin
An imprint of Penguin Random House LLC
penguinrandomhouse.com

Most Portfolio books are available at a discount when purchased in quantity for sales
promotions or corporate use. Special editions, which include personalized covers, excerpts,
and corporate imprints, can be created when purchased in large quantities. For more
information, please call (212) 572-2232 or e-mail specialmarkets@penguinrandomhouse.com.
Your local bookstore can also assist with discounted bulk purchases using the Penguin
Random House corporate Business-to-Business program. For assistance in locating
a participating retailer, e-mail B2B@penguinrandomhouse.com.

Insert p. 2 [bottom] by Jean Nichols; p. 3 [top and bottom] courtesy of CNN; p. 4 [top] by
Masatomo Kuriya / Corbis Premium Historical via Getty Images, [center and bottom]
courtesy of CNN; p. 5 [top, center, and bottom] courtesy of CNN; p. 6 [bottom]
courtesy © GaryMarlonSuson; p. 7 [center] by Jeff Kowalksy. Unless otherwise noted
all other photos courtesy of the author.

Library of Congress Cataloging-in-Publication Data
Names: Pfeifer, Joseph, 1956– author.
Title: Ordinary heroes : a memoir of 9/11 / Joseph Pfeifer.
Description: New York, NY : Portfolio/Penguin, [2021] | Includes
bibliographical references.
Identifiers: LCCN 2021024461 (print) | LCCN 2021024462 (ebook) |
ISBN 9780593330258 (hardcover) | ISBN 9780593330265 (ebook)
Subjects: LCSH: Pfeifer, Joseph, 1956– | New York (N.Y.). Fire Department. |
September 11 Terrorist Attacks, 2001. | Fire fighters—New York
(State)—New York—Biography. | Search and rescue operations—New York
(State)—New York. | Heroes—New York (State)—New York.
Classification: LCC HV6432.7 .P492 2021 (print) | LCC HV6432.7 (ebook) |
DDC 973.931—dc23
LC record available at https://lccn.loc.gov/2021024461
LC ebook record available at https://lccn.loc.gov/2021024462

Printed in the United States of America
1st Printing

BOOK DESIGN BY ELLEN CIPRIANO

MAP BY JEFFREY L. WARD

To the victims and survivors of extreme events throughout the world,
especially my brother Kevin Pfeifer, an FDNY Lieutenant in Engine 33,
and one of the 343 firefighters who died at the World Trade Center
on 9/11. And to all those who run into danger so others may live.
Your bravery is the inspiration for this book.

CONTENTS

ORDINARY
HEROES

1

AN ORDINARY DAY

IN THE SUMMER OF 2001, all of us in the Duane Street firehouse had been hoping for a real fire. What we got were smoke detectors going off in office buildings, a car fire or two, and a phone book aflame in a garbage can. Nothing exciting.

We didn't want a fire for the sake of a fire—we wanted one for Jules and Gédéon, and for Tony. For several months, Jules and Gédéon Naudet, two young French filmmakers, had been living at our firehouse on Duane Street. They were following Tony, a probationary firefighter—a "probie"—chosen during the three-month training academy of the Fire Department of the City of New York (FDNY). Their idea was to make a film portraying a "boy becoming a man in nine months"—the probation period when firefighters prove themselves.

And proving himself was what Antonios "Tony" Benetatos was eager to do. Unlike many probies, who had fathers or brothers in the department, Tony had no previous connection to the FDNY. He hadn't grown up in firefighter culture, but he had the drive for it. "It sounds kind of cheesy, but I always kinda wanted to be a hero," Tony had told Jules and Gédéon when they screened guys in the academy. "This is really the only thing you can do that you can do that."

On June 1, Tony had been assigned to 100 Duane Street. Home of Engine 7, Ladder 1, and Battalion 1, the Duane Street firehouse was one of New York's biggest and most historic firehouses. The Engine pumps water, and the Ladder, sometimes called the Truck, is a seventy-five-foot tower ladder. Founded in 1772, Ladder Company 1 predates the FDNY by almost one hundred years.

Probies learn to work both Engine and Ladder. After arriving at the scene of a fire, Ladder companies search for victims and locate the fire. Usually, the room is filled with smoke and you can't see your hand in front of your face. You search the room by keeping one hand on a wall, crawling and feeling for victims as you go, trying to sense heat, paying attention to how to get out fast if necessary.

While the Ladder searches, Engine companies hook up the hose to the hydrant, then stretch the hose from the pumper up the stairs to the location of the blaze. The Engine is a four-person team working the hose to extinguish the fire. What seems simple is a highly coordinated team effort. It takes four people to handle a hose. The nozzle firefighter directs the stream. Tony would have to learn it all, but for now he was on Engine 7. Teaching those skills and that mindset takes time and is the responsibility of the entire firehouse.

I was the battalion chief in charge of this firehouse and three other firehouses in lower Manhattan. Each fire company has one captain, three lieutenants, and about twenty-five firefighters.

A firehouse is very hierarchical. The captain is the head of the house, assisted by three lieutenants. The officer in charge of the unit, whether a captain or lieutenant, must account for everyone who is on the fire truck. The Engine chauffeur drives the rig to the scene and gets it set up near a hydrant to supply water to fire hoses. The Ladder chauffeur has to position the rig in front of the building, so if someone is on the roof or shows up at a window, they can be rescued. Officers and chauffeurs, with their firefighters, form a unit that looks out for each other as they carry out their mission to fight fires and save lives.

The guys and I welcomed Tony. Right away, he began fitting into firehouse life, checking equipment, washing the fire apparatus, cleaning pots, mopping floors, and practicing sliding down the fire pole, all the while waiting for his first real fire.

But things were slow when Tony was on duty. All we were doing was answering Class E alarms—smoke detectors going off in high-rises— and conducting building inspections. Though we had medical calls, we had no structural fires. Zero. After eight or nine weeks, Tony did get to put out one fire.

"I got to spray some water," Tony said with relief back at the firehouse. "I'm getting closer." He said "closer" because the fire had been a car ablaze on the Brooklyn Bridge.

"That's all right," firefighter Pat Zoda told him, patting his shoulder. "My first fire was a garbage can fire on West Broadway and Franklin."

If I thought back to my probie days, I could identify with Tony waiting for his first big test, his chance to prove to his fellow firefighters and himself that he could do the job. I could vividly recall one of my first fires in an occupied residence—entering the dark, smoke-filled room, finding the fire, putting it out—and understood his excitement and his trepidation.

And I could identify with his desire to be a hero. As a teenager, I'd been a lifeguard, a certified emergency medical technician (EMT), and a volunteer firefighter. I loved that sense of purpose, of knowing I was helping people who were in danger. We all did.

Captain Dennis Tardio of Engine 7 put it this way: "You need to get up in the morning and look at yourself in the mirror and say you are doing something with your life." For all of us in the firehouse, our jobs as firefighters provided just that sense of mission.

In FDNY lore, probies get dubbed "black clouds" or "white clouds." Black clouds bring fires, which keep the house busy doing the job firefighters love. White clouds bring no fires, no action, just boredom. Engine 7 Firefighter James Hanlon teased the frustrated Tony: "The kid is one very white cloud!"

Joking around was part of firehouse life, as a way to build trust in your team. One night, the guys lured Tony outside and dumped a bucket of water on his head. He looked peeved. A firefighter told Tony, "We're going to bust your chops till you laugh about it." Tony was being accepted, but, as Gédéon said, "The guys were not going to make it easy on him."

Neither were the fates that controlled fires. July and August passed without a fire for Tony. But after twenty years with the Fire Department of New York, five of those years as a battalion chief, I knew it was just a matter of time.

ON THE EVENING OF September 10, 2001, the aroma of roasting leg of lamb wafted up to my office from the firehouse kitchen, along with the sound of raucous laughter. The French guys were cooking.

I had arrived before 6 p.m., driving west from my home in Queens, across the Brooklyn Bridge to the firehouse at 100 Duane Street. That time of day, it usually took about forty-five minutes, and I enjoyed watching the sunset behind one of the most iconic views of the city: the Twin Towers with the Statue of Liberty in the distance.

Five days before, on September 5, I had celebrated my twentieth anniversary with the FDNY, becoming eligible for retirement. But leaving at age forty-five was unthinkable. I had studied hard to make battalion chief. I loved the job, as did my younger brother, Kevin. He'd joined the FDNY in 1991 and was now a lieutenant in Engine 33. His firehouse on Great Jones Street—a historic house built in 1899—was only a mile away from mine.

As brothers, Kevin and I were close. We lived in the same neighborhood where we grew up, Kevin only two houses away from my parents. My wife, Ginny, and I had bought a house a half dozen blocks away. Whenever we got together to sail, barbecue, or just hang out, Kevin and I talked about firefighting. We both loved the department and working downtown. Still single, he enjoyed the nightlife and exploring the city.

Firefighting had brought Kevin and me even closer together. The FDNY was our family in a way most jobs are not. The department fostered a close-knit atmosphere with picnics, barbecues, Christmas celebrations, and recognition dinners for firefighters and their families. Firefighters helped each other with household projects, big and small. Spouses got to know each other. Kids were welcome at the firehouse. We formed study groups to prepare for promotion tests. In a world where many have only a handful of good friends, we had dozens. Firefighting was our way of life.

It was fate I was at the firehouse that night. I typically worked two nine-hour day tours with forty-eight hours off, then two fifteen-hour night tours followed by seventy-two hours off. However, we could do a mutual exchange of tours and work twenty-four hours straight. Another chief in the battalion needed to be off and asked me to do a "mutual" swap, meaning I'd work from 6 p.m. on September 10 until 6 p.m. the next day. I thought nothing of it and readily agreed.

Though my office and quarters were at the Duane Street firehouse, I had management responsibilities for four firehouses. During my twenty-four-hour tour, I'd check in with the other three as well: Ten House—the firehouse of Engine 10, Ladder 10—was located on Liberty Street across from the World Trade Center; historic Engine 6 at 49 Beekman Street, located by City Hall and sporting the enormous image of a tiger's head painted on its main door; and the South Street firehouse, Engine 4, Ladder 15, near Wall Street.

I loved being a battalion chief. For the first time in my career, I wasn't focused on advancement. I had found the perfect rank, which combined commanding at fires from Canal Street to the very tip of Manhattan and connecting during meals with the guys in the firehouses, hearing their stories, especially about big fires.

Each night, in every firehouse in every borough of New York, firefighters eat a hearty dinner together. Firefighters are great cooks, and preparing and eating meals together builds camaraderie. After a fire or other emergency response, everyone sits around the enormous kitchen table to talk about what we did and what we'd do differently next time. Telling stories, especially after a demanding experience, is part of learning as much as it is about friendship.

Tonight, when I got to the firehouse, it wasn't firefighters cooking, though. It was Jules and Gédéon, the French filmmakers.

The firefighters hadn't made it easy for the Naudet brothers—the "frogs," as they called them. Half the firefighters refused to talk to them for weeks after they moved in on June 1. Others dropped their pants, shot them the finger, or cursed with colorful and over-the-top profanity whenever Gédéon's camera was rolling. But thirty-one-year-old Gédéon just kept filming.

In August, Jules, who was twenty-eight, mentioned their frustration to his grandmother. She told her grandson, who had learned his way around the kitchen at her knee, to "start cooking." Jules took her advice and got to work. He made fresh *pommes frites* and lasagna for communal meals, and slowly the guys warmed up.

To show their gratitude to the firehouse for embracing them, on the night of September 10, Jules took over the kitchen to make his specialty—roast leg of lamb—for thirteen very hungry firefighters. Mouths watered in anticipation.

I stayed out of the kitchen; officers are not allowed near the stove. That's the firefighters' domain—a sign of respect as well as defining people's roles. If an officer even tries to wash a pot—or touch a hose—firefighters will wrestle it from their hands.

As Jules and Gédéon cooked, everyone talked. They chatted about fires, about family life, about what we were going to do tomorrow. The meal tasted fantastic but fell spectacularly short in quantity. Firefighters eat fast—because they may have to run out to a fire—and have huge appetites. The thin slices of Jules's perfectly cooked lamb, roast potatoes, and vegetables disappeared in minutes.

"That's all we get?" one strapping firefighter complained. "That's not even a snack!" For the rest of the evening, the guys taunted the brothers for roasting only one leg of lamb instead of four, gnawing on the huge bones as if they were starving cavemen.

"Where's Frenchie?" said firefighter Kirk Pritchard. "A couple more meals like this, and we'll be able to share shirts."

"All right, all right, I got a small piece," Jules said, hanging his head. "My mistake."

To rub it in, the firefighters later ordered pizza. "We had a great time," Gédéon said later. "We were getting accepted." In a way, they were also probies. They slept in the firehouse and sometimes sat "housewatch"—to monitor the computer for calls and listen to surrounding fires on the department radio. But they were frustrated and discouraged on a professional level.

"By the end of August, we knew that we had a great cooking show," Gédéon said, "and there were no fires." But as Jules said, "Every time we would talk with some of the senior guys, they always told us—well, be careful what you wish for."

It's always dangerous when a firehouse hits a long dry spell. According to an old firehouse legend, when it ends, you'll get a really big one.

Tony had already gotten a glimpse of the very real risks. On the first day of September, he and thousands of other members of the FDNY had attended the funeral of a rookie firefighter from Staten Island who'd died of a heart attack during a blaze after only a few months on the job, leaving behind a two-year-old son and a wife with a baby on the way. Tony was given the sobering task of lowering the firehouse flag to half-staff in the rookie's honor.

I enjoyed Jules's lamb dinner with the rest of the guys, then returned to my office to do some paperwork. I never slept at the firehouse, only occasionally resting my eyes between runs. That night, we had several— a smoke detector going off in a high-rise—but nothing requiring putting "the wet stuff on the red stuff," as firefighters liked to say.

2

AIMING FOR
THE NORTH TOWER

THE MORNING AFTER the lamb dinner, loud chatter and the smell of coffee filled the firehouse. Firefighters bustled around the kitchen, cracking eggs and frying bacon. Jules and Gédéon were still getting razzed about the lamb dinner, especially by some of the bigger guys. But they took it in stride, happy to be teased.

I ate breakfast with the outgoing crew and those coming on for the next tour, which started at 9 a.m. after morning roll call. I had worked fifteen hours and had another nine to go. Despite not having slept, I wasn't all that tired. I was used to this kind of shift, and the long hours didn't bother me.

I'd called my wife, Ginny, the night before, as I usually did. An oncology nurse, Ginny was off that day. We alternated shifts so one of us could always stay at home with our children—Christine, age fifteen, and Greg, age twelve. When I worked, she would boast about having the whole bed to herself, but we couldn't wait to be together when my shift ended.

At 8:33 a.m., we got the call to respond to a "possible odor of gas" about seven blocks north of the firehouse. Firefighters gulped the last of their breakfast coffee and grabbed their helmets and bunker gear. Guys still upstairs slid down the firehouse pole.

Nobody got excited. It was a routine emergency, one of the most common calls to the firehouse. Each person goes to their designated spot on the apparatus.

Captain Dennis Tardio hopped on Engine 7, which carries hose, nozzles, and connections to standpipes. He was joined by Engine Company Chauffeur Tom Spinard, who had the important responsibility of correctly positioning the engine at hydrants when we arrived at a fire scene, making sure that the water pressure was maintained. Firefighters Jamal Braithwaite, Joe Casaliggi, and Pat Zoda took their usual spots on the rig.

Lieutenant Bill Walsh did the same with Ladder 1, which carries the various tools we use to force entry or to check for fire spread. Ladder Company Chauffeur John O'Neill got behind the wheel, as Firefighters Nick Borrillo, Damian Van Cleaf, Steve Olsen, and Hank Ryan climbed into their seats.

Jules, who had started riding along with me on most shifts in the battalion chief's vehicle, jumped into the backseat of my red Suburban with its rack of flashing lights. Gédéon was usually the one who rode in the Engine and did the filming, while Jules assisted him with logistics. But Gédéon had urged Jules to learn how to shoot as well, and in August, they had bought a second camera. That morning, Jules rode with me to practice filming for one more run before heading home after the long night.

The FDNY dispatcher sent us to the northeast corner of Church and Lispenard Streets in Tribeca. We'd meet Ladder 8 at the scene and Engine 6 was en route. We were responding with two Engines, two Ladders, and a battalion chief, a typical response for an odor of gas because of the fear of an explosion.

Arriving in three minutes, we dismounted the rigs into a glorious September morning: pristine blue sky, bright sun, mild temperature, summer just heading into fall—one of those "top ten" days of the year that makes you feel alive, ready to tackle anything.

Standing in the street, I pulled out a gas detector about the size of a firefighter's portable radio with a very sensitive probe on the top, which I carried in my vehicle. After a few minutes walking up and down the street, I got a buzzing sound, a hit, over a sewer grate, and a whiff of sewer gas, a normal false positive. I sent some firefighters into basements and nearby restaurants, looking for the source, and they found none. As was standard practice, I asked my aide to contact Con Ed to check it out with their equipment.

Suddenly, I heard the thunderous roar of jet engines at full throttle. In Manhattan, you rarely hear planes because of the tall buildings. Looking west, I saw a low-flying commercial airliner so close that I could read the word "American" on the fuselage. Racing south above the Hudson River, visible just above the buildings on Church Street, the plane zoomed past us and disappeared from my sight for a couple of seconds behind some taller buildings.

When it reappeared, I saw the aircraft was aiming for the North Tower of the World Trade Center.

It was 8:46 a.m.

I stood on the street and watched as the airplane intentionally crashed into the upper floors of the World Trade Center. The aircraft slammed dead center into the building, the wings carving a huge gash through the upper floors of the 110-story skyscraper. A massive fireball erupted, followed a second later by an earsplitting explosion. Black smoke billowed from the wound the aircraft had ripped in the steel and glass building.

The impact took my breath away. Time seemed to stand still as we watched the flames. Then the firefighters around me erupted in a chorus of, "Holy shit! Oh my God! Holy shit! A plane hit the building!"

In horror and disbelief, I tried to comprehend what I had just seen. One of the tallest buildings in the world was struck by a commercial jet and on fire. Thousands of people were in that building or arriving to begin their workday. We were only a few blocks from the World Trade Center, almost certainly some of the closest firefighters to the disaster. As the closest chief in lower Manhattan, I knew instantly I was going to be the first chief on the scene and would have to take command.

"Get back on the rigs!" shouted Captain Tardio to Engine 7's firefighters, who grabbed their equipment and scrambled into their places on the vehicles. Lieutenant Walsh did the same thing with the firefighters of Ladder 1.

I jumped back into my red SUV, followed by Jules. "Go, go to the Trade Center," I told firefighter Ed Fahey, who that day was driving me for the first time as a battalion aide. His job was to drive with lights and sirens, so I could talk on the department radio.

I looked up at the smoking North Tower and grabbed the radio. I needed to give concise orders to command and control our response.

"Battalion 1 to Manhattan."

"Battalion 1," the dispatcher responded.

"We just had a plane crash into upper floors of the World Trade Center," I said. "Transmit a second alarm and start relocating companies into the area."

"Ten-four, Battalion 1."

"Battalion 1 is also sending the whole assignment on this box to that area." I was informing the dispatcher that the units with me at the odor of gas were now assigned to the WTC. "This box" referred to the location of the red fire callbox on the corner. All the rigs on that box were now heading to Box 8087, the North Tower of the World Trade Center.

With lights flashing and sirens blaring, our convoy raced south on West Broadway to the WTC.

In seconds my mind flooded with a hundred pieces of information as I thought about my next moves. Fighting thousands of fires had taught me to recognize danger, to pick up small details and process them at lightning speed. The more experience you have, the faster you can process the information by matching it to past incidents and envision a possible course of action. But this was a novel event. I had to slow my thinking down and anticipate the unexpected.

"That was an American Airlines plane," I said. "That looked like a direct attack." I had no idea who was responsible, but I knew it was a terrorist attack. I could feel my heart rate subtly increase.

At the height of the workday, there were as many as 40,000 people in the World Trade Center complex. Hundreds of people had probably died as the plane bulldozed through the building. Many others were likely in danger. Of one thing, I was certain: we were going to the biggest fire of our lifetime, the biggest fire since the FDNY was founded in 1865. I was in charge of the FDNY response for now. I had to gather situational awareness, inform the dispatcher, request additional alarms, develop a plan, and deploy firefighting resources.

As we drove, I watched white and black smoke billowing from the building. After the initial fireball, I saw no more flame. It was difficult to identify exactly which floors were involved, but certainly, multiple floors were now internally ablaze and the fire would quickly spread.

Over the years as a firefighter, I had learned how important it was in a crisis to be flexible in my thought processes. I learned when to rely on intuitive gut feelings—*That wall is about to collapse! Get out!*—and when to switch to deliberate or analytical thinking. Especially as a chief, being able to step back and see the big picture is crucial.

I forced myself into a deliberate calm. Though I had extensive experience with high-rise fires and taught the subject at the fire academy, none of us had ever been confronted with a massive high-rise fire on numerous upper floors. My focus was: *What do I need to do right now?*

Sixty seconds after giving the first radio transmission, I got on the radio again.

"Battalion 1 to Manhattan . . . We have a number of floors on fire. It looked like the plane was aiming toward the building. Transmit a third alarm. We'll have the staging area at Vesey and West Street. Have the third alarm assignment go into that area, the second alarm assignment to report to the building."

The dispatcher and the incoming units needed to know what I knew in my gut: this was not an accident but a deliberate attack by a plane aiming for the building. With those two orders, I had asked for about 150 firefighters to go to the scene, with two-thirds reporting to me in the building, others reporting to a staging location where they would await assignment.

I HAD A FEW MINUTES to think as Fahey drove. I knew the World Trade Center well, especially being a battalion chief in Battalion 1, whose response area was the tip of Manhattan, including the WTC, Wall Street, the Statue of Liberty, and Ellis Island.

On any tour of duty, I might visit the sixteen-acre WTC complex several times. Thanks to years of experience, I was familiar with the

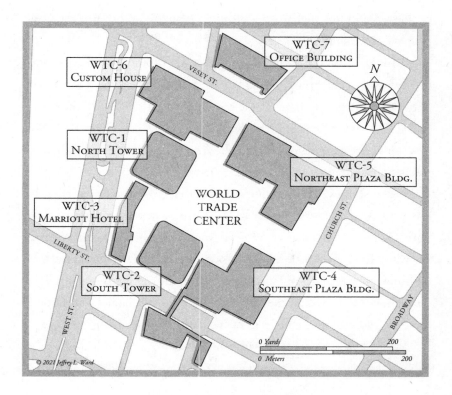

layouts and fire safety systems of each of the seven buildings: the North (WTC-1) and South (WTC-2) Towers, the Marriott Hotel (WTC-3), the Southeast Plaza Building (WTC-4), the Northeast Plaza Building (WTC-5), the Custom House (WTC-6), and a 47-story office building (WTC-7).

This wasn't the first time the World Trade Center had faced a terrorist attack. On February 26, 1993, an extremist had parked a rental van stuffed with explosives in an underground parking garage of the WTC. It blasted a hundred-foot-wide crater through four subfloors, knocking out the center's elevators, public-address system, and electricity lines. Six people were killed, including a pregnant woman, and over a thousand people had been injured.

A month after the 1993 bombing, I made captain and was assigned to midtown Manhattan. Promoted in a time when the FDNY and NYPD were working hard to fix the vulnerabilities the attack had revealed, I'd spent a lot of time studying skyscraper fires. This was a whole new world of firefighting for me. The fires were more complex, hard to reach, and sometimes hard to find.

In my studies and subsequent years of fighting skyscraper fires, I'd learned that the biggest danger to most people in a high-rise fire is not burns, but smoke inhalation. When a fire is controlled in a one- to three-story building, you break windows to let smoke escape. That is not wise with most high-rise fires; falling glass can injure civilians and firefighters. Without that release, the smoke builds up, often fatally—it obscures the exits and starves the lungs of oxygen, killing you within minutes.

We had to get people out fast, but I wasn't sure we would be fast enough. I had designed a training exercise on the 93rd floor of the WTC South Tower in 1999. Even with working elevators in an empty building, it had taken twenty minutes to get firefighters up to the 93rd floor. That had not taken into account a commercial airliner laden with jet fuel, used as a terrorists' missile against a high-rise building, igniting infernos on multiple floors.

Knowing every second counted for the people trapped in the building, we raced south, passing pedestrians who had stopped to look up, stare, and point, mouths agape. At 8:50 a.m., we arrived at the North Tower on the West Street side. The rigs of Ten House, a block away, arrived at the same time. Smoke was pouring out of the upper heights of the building as ash and paper drifted down. Chunks of glass littered the ground outside the building.

"Pull over," I told Fahey at the driveway to the lobby doors, allowing Engine 7 to take a hydrant and pump water into the building's sprinkler and standpipe system. Fahey pulled under the Plexiglas porte cochere in front of the building to avoid the falling wreckage. Ladder 1 parked on the street in front.

Guys piled off their rigs, grabbing hose and tools.

I jumped out while Fahey stayed in my car to monitor radio traffic. Division 1 Deputy Chief Peter Hayden was on his way. Fahey would join me when DC Hayden arrived.

My bunker gear was in the back of the vehicle. I climbed into the heavy knee-high leather boots, pulled the bunker pants over my slacks, then shrugged into the bulky black turnout coat made of Nomex, a heat- and flame-resistant fabric. It had reflective yellow stripes and my rank and last name across the back of the coat.

I put on the white helmet that identified me as a battalion chief at fire scenes. But I left my self-contained breathing apparatus (SCBA) in the vehicle. A face mask attached to an air tank, the SCBA weighed twenty pounds that I didn't need to carry.

"Can I come with you, Chief?" asked Jules. He was wearing jeans, sneakers, and an FDNY T-shirt. Most other people would have run away, but Jules was now part of the firehouse on Duane Street, and the lobby is usually safe when the fire is many floors above.

"Yeah, you stay with me," I said. "I want you right next to me. Never leave my side."

I looked up at the tower and saw smoke churning. But I was seeing only the west side of the building. The plane had struck from the north. I knew there had to be an inferno inside.

My plan was to urgently mobilize resources, evacuate all occupants, and rescue those who could not get out. Save life first, contain the flames, and then we'd think about extinguishing the fire. However, I needed to send up engine companies with rolled-up hose to attach to the standpipe water supply, figuring that we may have to extinguish fire to get to people who were trapped.

Before sending anyone up, I needed to gather information on what was being reported about conditions above.

The soaring six-story lobby, usually festooned with colorful flags of the world, looked like it had been hit by a bomb. The thick floor-to-ceiling windows on two sides of the lobby had been shattered. Shards of glittering glass littered the floors. Large white-and-gray marble panels had crashed from the walls and lay in broken chunks. One entire bank of elevators had been destroyed by the initial fireball racing down the shaft and exploding into the lobby. But the lights were still functioning. The large space had a faint smell of jet fuel but was clear of smoke.

At 8:50 a.m., as we entered the doors to the lobby, we saw a man and woman who had collapsed on the floor of the entryway, skin charred, some of their clothing still on fire. The woman was screaming. They'd been badly burned by a fireball.

"I'll put them out," Firefighter Jamal Braithwaite told Captain Tardio.

"Yeah," Tardio told him. EMS ambulances that were close behind would treat and transport the patients to the hospital. Braithwaite grabbed a fire extinguisher and smothered the flames.

Tardio and Jules followed me inside, along with the firefighters of Engines 7 and 10 and Ladders 1, 8, and 10.

Inside were other civilians who had been burned. As awful as it was to see them suffer, I knew I could not stop to help them. Firefighters and EMTs right behind me would provide medical care. My job was to take command of this event, to rescue the hundreds of people who were trapped.

Lloyd Thomas, one of the Port Authority fire safety directors, ran up to me. "The plane hit the top of the building. Looks like the fires are somewhere above the 78th floor." This was the best information he had. The building's fire detection system had been knocked out.

Thomas told me that a full building evacuation order had been given on the intercom within one minute of the building being hit. People had started coming down and were being directed to exit at the mezzanine level.

I was glad to hear that many were evacuating safely, but we had to assume we had a thousand people trapped above the fire. In addition to the 10,000 people who worked in the North Tower, hundreds of others came for meetings or to visit the renowned Windows on the World restaurant on the 106th and 107th floors. The restaurant had probably already opened for business. The only good news was that perhaps many people had not yet arrived for work or meetings.

I turned left and proceeded to the fire command station in the lobby, which had a long, chest-high marble partition separating the public from the fire safety panel, phones, and desk, so I could gather information about the building's systems and possible location of the fire.

I ordered Captain Tardio, who had twenty-two years of experience and knew the WTC well: "Find me working elevators." Without elevators, rescuers would have to climb the narrow four-foot-wide stairs. With bunker gear, SCBAs, search rope, roll-ups of fifty feet of hose, and other equipment such as axes and Halligan tools, firefighters would have to haul at least sixty pounds up each flight. They would have to get around people evacuating down the stairs—not a good situation when we needed to move fast.

Tardio and members of Engine 7 fanned out with their firefighters' service keys to recall the elevators to the lobbies.

Each tower had ninety-nine elevators. Large-capacity express elevators went up to sky lobbies on the 44th and 78th floors, where people took smaller elevators to higher floors. A few minutes later, a grim-looking Tardio returned. The unit hadn't found even one functional elevator in the North Tower.

I asked an official with the Port Authority to call each elevator, to see if people were trapped inside, and to ask if they knew what floors they were stuck on or between. We'd send someone up to get them out with tools. In the far corner of the fire command station, he started to call each elevator, asking anyone inside to yell or kick the doors so firefighters could locate them.

FDNY dispatchers had been flooded with distress calls from people who were injured, burned, or trapped on upper floors. People in wheelchairs couldn't get out because the elevators weren't working. One report said thirty people were on the 40th floor, some severely injured and in need of assistance.

Within six minutes of my arrival, Mike Hurley, the fire safety director of the WTC complex, asked if I wanted to evacuate the South Tower.

The South Tower hadn't been hit, but the entire complex would be affected by such a large fire in the North Tower. "Yes, evacuate the South Tower," I said, handing him the desk phone at the fire command. "Do it now. Let's get everyone down." People could exit through the underground part of the complex to avoid falling debris. Hurley immediately relayed my evacuation order to the safety directors in the South Tower.

I had ordered the evacuation of both towers. Things were happening rapidly. With the elevators unusable, it was a race against time to get up to those who were trapped.

3

———

GO UP

T HE HUGE LOBBY OF THE North Tower was filling up as firefight-ers arrived and awaited assignment. Each officer approached to let me know they and their units were available. Most people just walked in through the broken windows. But it was not chaotic, just solemn faces entering an unfolding crisis, waiting to be told what to do.

Firefighters aren't the quietest people in the world. At most fires, there's loud chitchat, orders being given, and colorful language. But this morning, the lobby was a grim place. They entered with grave concern on their faces. They saw the burning towers and knew they were going to the most dangerous fire of their careers.

People were trapped and needed our help. It was our job, but each of us made a personal decision to go in and risk our lives for others.

At 8:55 a.m., Deputy Chief Hayden entered the lobby. Hayden had been at his quarters in SoHo, the firehouse at Lafayette and Spring, when he heard a plane passing overhead, extremely low and loud. He ran to a window in time to hear the impact, though the buildings obscured his line of sight. Hayden suspected a plane had accidentally crashed some-where in lower Manhattan. When the chief heard me call for multiple alarms to the WTC on the radio, he grabbed his aide and said, "Let's go."

During his drive down Lafayette Street, Hayden saw only a huge column of smoke, no flame, giving him little information about where the fire was blazing. But he immediately ordered FDNY Hazmat and Rescue specialty units to respond.

On his arrival, Hayden became the incident commander. I was glad to see him. Hayden was the quintessential FDNY firefighter. Born of Irish parents, he grew up in Rockaway, Queens, joined the FDNY in 1968, and had a brother, two sons, and a son-in-law in the department. We'd worked fires together for many years and knew how each other thought. Pete was a person of action and always wanted things done quickly. I was more analytical and could anticipate the outcomes of our decisions. Together, we had a half century of experience in the FDNY and were both very familiar with the WTC complex.

I brought Hayden up to speed with what I knew, which was still precious little. Whatever floors were involved, the body of fire was large and growing fast, fueled by office combustibles—material like desks, chairs, paper files, and other furnishings.

In front of the fire panel, we set up a magnetic command board brought by Hayden, like a big aluminum suitcase with fold-down legs. With its battered top propped up, you could see the words "Command Post" and an FDNY logo. His aide, Firefighter Christian Waugh, started tracking units using numbered chips in different colors, which designated whether a unit was Engine, Ladder, Rescue, Squad, Hazmat, or Battalion. The board design dated back to World War II; it was effective, if primitive. We could see at a glance which units had been deployed where.

Hayden and I agreed that evacuation and rescue would be our priority.

We had to get the people out of the building. I saw Jim Corrigan, retired captain of Ten House, now one of the Port Authority fire safety directors, and asked him to put his engineers to work on gaining control of the building's systems, especially the elevators. Without working elevators, our rescue operations would be slowed considerably as rescuers would have to climb the narrow stairs in this gigantic skyscraper.

Three to six firefighters, with their heavy gear, would go up as a unit, led by a fire officer. Fire officers carry only a big flashlight and an eighteen-inch officer's tool that resembles a small crowbar. They direct units and evaluate risk, keeping their firefighters safe. If something doesn't feel right, they pull them out. The officers would be the first to go into danger as they led their teams for search and rescue. But they couldn't race ahead of their unit. The officer and firefighters were a team.

At first, aggressive firefighters might climb one floor per minute. But after ten flights, exertion and equipment would slow that down to perhaps two minutes a floor. That might slow further as they found injured people in the stairwell, were blocked by debris, or encountered smoke or flame. Just to get up to the floor below the fire could take over an hour.

That gave me pause. But people needed us.

The simplicity of the structure would seem to be an advantage. Each of the tower's 110 floors was square, with each side of the building measuring 208 feet in length, about one acre of open space per floor. Stairwells A, B, and C were situated in the center core of the building, where all the electrical conduits, water pipes, and elevators were located. The three stairwells, elevator banks, and utilities fit like a smaller square inside the bigger square.

But they weren't exactly the same. Stairwells A and C ran from the mezzanine level of the lobby up to the 110th floor. Stairwell B ran from

B6 in the basement up to the 107th floor, accessible from the West Street lobby area, where we had entered that morning. But stairs A and C had deviations to transfer hallways, which could be confusing to people unfamiliar with them. Those had caused confusion during the 1993 evacuation.

In each stairwell, there was a standpipe, or water main, which ran the height of the building. Each floor had a spout with a wheel. The wheel controlled the water pressure. Once firefighters reached the floors involved with the fire, they could use water to cut a path through flames to reach those trapped.

At 8:57 a.m., seven minutes after our arrival, I gave orders to Captain Tardio to take Engine 7 and climb up toward the impact zone, checking each floor for civilians and fire before continuing up. I didn't want them to get trapped on a higher floor with a growing fire beneath them. But they were to go no higher than the 70th floor. Eight floors below the fires was a reasonable margin of safety.

They were to report conditions they encountered by radio. We didn't know whether stairwells were filling with smoke, didn't know the impact floors, and didn't know if water for firefighting would be available on upper levels. We were making critical choices with little to no information. We had no video feed allowing us to see the exterior of the building.

Without hesitation, Tardio, carrying an extra length of hose, turned and led the men of Engine 7 toward the staircase. They were followed by Lieutenant Walsh leading Ladder 1, with orders to go up any staircase that was available, help any civilians who needed it, and give us a report by radio.

Battalion 7 Chief Orio Palmer and his units arrived from their quarters in Chelsea on the west side of Manhattan. About the same age, Palmer and I had been captains in neighboring firehouses in a heavily populated area of Corona and Jackson Heights in Queens. Both highly competitive, we ran in fire department races against each other.

Promoted to battalion chief about the same time, we had spent hours discussing the challenges of radio communications in high-rise firefighting. We used analog, point-to-point radios that had six normal operating channels. Companies would operate on the same tactical channel, which chiefs like me would monitor and use to communicate with firefighters in an emergency. The chiefs had a separate command channel to communicate with each other.

But these radios had weak signal strength and often didn't penetrate the steel and concrete floors separating companies attempting to talk to each other. When many companies were trying to use the same channel at the same time, communications became unintelligible.

After the 1993 bombing, the Port Authority had installed a repeater system on the roof of WTC-5 to boost FDNY radio communications in the complex. The radio signal would be received by the repeater at a low wattage on one frequency and transmitted on another frequency at a higher wattage. An activation console was installed in the fire safety desk of each tower.

Chief Palmer and I had trained many times on the WTC's system, used only for the chiefs' command channel. Because it interfered with our operations in lower Manhattan, we asked them to keep the repeater off unless it was needed. When I first arrived, I had asked Lloyd Thomas, the civilian safety director for the building, to turn the repeater on.

Chief Hayden and I began ordering more units up. Some we sent to respond to particular distress calls. We had reports of civilians with chest pains or in wheelchairs. One blind woman needed help to get down the stairs. I told one battalion chief and three companies to clear floors 21 to 25, then continue up, but no higher than the 70th-floor staging area.

One fire lieutenant from Engine 33 came up to me. I was surprised to see him. It was my brother Kevin, and he was supposed to be off studying for the captain's exam. Without saying a word, he and I looked at each other, wondering if the other was going to be okay. Then I ordered him to take his company and "go up the B stairs to the 70th floor and evacuate occupants along the way."

My brother slowly turned and quietly led his Engine 33 firefighters—David Arce, Michael Boyle, Robert Evans, Robert King, and Keithroy Maynard—to a stairwell.

We still had no information from the outside, nothing even as simple as what floors were involved. Within minutes of Chief Hayden's arrival, police helicopters began circling the towers. We wanted to know if we could do a helicopter roof rescue. One of the other chiefs had grabbed my citywide radio, so I tried a landline to get through to the FDNY dispatcher. I kept trying but could get no response. However, at 8:58 a.m., an NYPD helicopter pilot radioed to their dispatcher that they could not do any roof rescue because of smoke and heat. This meant that the only way to get to people was from the interior.

Sounds of sirens filled the streets outside the lobby as emergency units continued to stream into the area. The entire FDNY hierarchy had mobilized. Responding from headquarters in Brooklyn were Chief of Department Pete Ganci, Jr., Chief of Operations Daniel Nigro, Assistant Chief Sal Cassano, and other high-ranking chiefs. Ganci set up the Incident Command Post (ICP) across from the North Tower on the far side of West Street, a six-lane street in front of the World Financial Center. From that safe vantage point, he could look at the big picture strategically and coordinate the massive resources, communications, and operations needed to respond to this unprecedented event.

A Port Authority police officer passed me news that people were trapped in elevators, but he did not have exact locations. The building staff continued fielding desperate calls from people begging for help on the intercom phones.

I thought about my brother. Kevin and other fire officers had started the long slog up the stairs, leading their teams. What would they encounter?

THE DUANE STREET FIREFIGHTERS WITH Engine 7 and Ladder 1 approached their assignments to go up the stairs with the conviction that their mission would succeed.

"I felt the mood that we were gonna put the fire out," said Firefighter Damian Van Cleaf, of Ladder 1. "Everyone seemed to be confident. I know I was."

"You basically looked at it and said, Okay, we got ten to twenty stories of fire," said Captain Tardio, of Engine 7. "We'll deal with it. We'll get up there; we'll get to it."

Tardio had spent his first eleven years at a house in Chinatown. As a lieutenant, he worked in Staten Island, bounced around Brooklyn for a few years as a captain, before coming back to Manhattan and getting assigned to Engine 7. A leader who took his role of training and drilling the younger firefighters very seriously, he'd get to the firehouse early to relieve the offgoing officer and get ready for his tour, well before he was due.

Standing on the street at the odor of gas call, Tardio looked up and saw the first airplane heading toward the North Tower. In mounting horror, he said to himself, "Turn, turn," trying to will the pilot to change course. "And he hit it, as if there was a bull's-eye on it."

Within seconds, he was shouting to the men to get on the rigs.

As he watched the impact, thirty-year-old Van Cleaf felt as if someone had taken "the air and sucked it out of my lungs and my head. I became so light-headed, my knees buckled and it felt like a dream as I saw the plane crumble into the building and just disintegrate."

Arriving at the WTC, Tardio instructed his chauffeur, Tommy Spinard, to make sure he could get a hydrant near the building's sprinkler standpipe. Spinard hooked up to the hydrant by the curb, which wasn't protected by the overhang, stretched three lengths of hose, and started pumping at 200 pounds of pressure.

Spinard saw injured civilians lying in the street. Two naked women sat on a grass divider in the middle of West Street, gray from head to toe. Their clothes had been burned off. They were still alive, but just staring, not moving. Firefighter Casaliggi made eye contact with one of the women and he went numb. As an EMT, he wondered if they were going to do medical treatment. He ran to the other side of the rig and told Tardio, "Captain, we got bodies in the street."

Tardio calmly said, "Get the roll-ups." An EMS ambulance arrived and took the injured people away.

After ascertaining the elevators weren't working, Tardio and Firefighters Braithwaite and Pat Zoda started up stairwell C. Tardio grabbed an extra roll of hose himself. Though not a big guy, he was carrying, with his bunker gear, close to sixty pounds of weight. They started up the stairs, which were so narrow there was room only for two people to pass, one going up while another was going down. He knew they were walking into hell, but the only thing going through his mind was, "We have to get up there."

As they climbed the stairway, they encountered civilians coming down in a steady stream, some injured or burned, with their clothes and skin hanging off. They tried to comfort them, to tell them it would be all right, to stay calm but get out as quickly as possible. *Don't stop!* They found a scorched woman just sitting in the C staircase, clearly in shock, unable to move on her own. They put her with a group of firefighters to take her down.

Civilians who passed were glad to see them. "They were pretty much saying, 'God bless you' and 'I can't believe y'all are going up and we're coming down,'" Braithwaite, of Engine 7, said. "People pretty much said, 'Why y'all going up there—get out!'"

But none of the firefighters turned around. As they climbed, they sweated from the exertion of carrying their gear. People were overheating, getting thirsty.

They asked everyone about what they had seen on higher floors. Was there fire? Tardio didn't want to pass a small blaze, then discover as they got higher that it had grown and was blocking their descent. On each floor, they quickly searched to make sure everyone had left.

Walsh and Ladder 1 were not far behind Tardio and Engine 7, going up stairwell B.

Walsh had arrived that morning at about 7:30 a.m. and did paperwork for about an hour before the odor of gas call. When Walsh saw the American Airlines jet, he assumed the pilot was in trouble, that he was going to veer off and ditch into the harbor.

When the aircraft instead crashed into the building, creating a gaping hole six stories high, Walsh instantly knew "we had a tough twenty-four-hour tour ahead of us. And the unexpected was gonna happen . . . We've never experienced something like this before." He anticipated having to walk up ninety flights of stairs before they could get to the fire.

Ladder 1 Chauffeur John O'Neill raced toward the WTC, swerving to avoid debris in the road. A veteran of the response to the 1993 bombing, O'Neill had been chatting with the chauffeur of Ladder 8 and hadn't taken much notice of the plane at first, just saw a silver blur against the blue sky. Then he heard the sound, turned around, and saw the building had been hit and flames had erupted in the hole.

"Right then and there, I knew this was going to be the worst day of my life as a firefighter," O'Neill said. "And it gave me a chill right down into my bones. It wasn't that queasy feeling that you get in your stomach. This one went right to my marrow immediately. In that second, I already knew that there were a lot of dead people up there. And possibly going to be even more. And it really shook me full of tremendous fear. Fear for myself and fear for the people who were up there." It was a feeling he'd never before had as a firefighter.

But O'Neill didn't tell the others that. Privately, he knew they were in for a marathon, not a sprint. He and Lieutenant Walsh jumped back on their rig, along with Firefighters Van Cleaf, Borrillo, Olsen, and Ryan.

"Well, we have our hands full here," O'Neill told Walsh as he drove. "We're just gonna do it."

Driving down West Street, looking at the smoke pouring from the building, O'Neill hoped he would wake up from the nightmare. But he controlled his fear, telling his crew, "Nice and easy, guys. Take it easy," as if sensing a need to calm their jitters. After parking the rig, he joined his team inside.

When Walsh first took his men to stairwell B at my direction, so many people were coming down that they had to wait a few minutes for the traffic to slow. Though the B stairwell was congested, people were walking down in an orderly, controlled fashion. The firefighters asked each group where they had been when the plane hit. The highest anyone mentioned was the 80th floor.

Walsh noticed Steve Olsen going ahead of the group, which he didn't like. He didn't want anyone freelancing. Anticipating they might have to climb ninety floors, Walsh knew they needed to pace themselves.

"We knew it was going to be a long haul getting up there," said Nick Borrillo, of Ladder 1. "Had to try to conserve as much energy as I could getting up there. But that was impossible."

As they passed the steady stream of occupants, O'Neill wondered how they could accomplish anything. He believed there would be a problem with the water supply due to the damage the jet had caused. Multiple floors had initially looked to be involved in the fire, but he knew that was spreading quickly. "In a building like that, it was almost impossible to put out with the kinds of means that we would have at that point." But O'Neill didn't air his opinion.

By the time Ladder 1 hit the 19th floor, Walsh had to wait on Van Cleaf to catch up. But he acquired a new guy, a straggler with Ladder 10, who had gotten separated from his group. It wasn't a good environment to be operating alone. Walsh was worried about Firefighter Olsen, who had told him by handie-talkie that he had made it up to the 22nd floor.

"Wait for me," Walsh told him. "Don't go any further."

The company plus one entered one of the offices on the west side of the building to take a break. They took off their turnout coats and helmets and SCBAs and sat down. Everyone was sweating heavily. Someone broke into a vending machine for water bottles, juice, and cookies.

Walsh heard a mayday from Engine 5, taking a break on the east side of the 19th floor. A firefighter was having a heart attack. An EMT, Walsh went to check on the man, who was having chest pains. They called for oxygen, but the firefighter recovered after resting.

Meanwhile, Casaliggi, of Engine 7, was stuck outside. He had initially followed Captain Tardio into the building while Spinard remained outside with the rig alone amid escalating chaos as rigs, ambulances, and cop cars raced to the scene. After Casaliggi returned to the rig for a replacement for a malfunctioning air cylinder, he stayed to help Spinard, watching for falling hazards as the chauffeur handled the fire pumps. Debris rained down: chunks of glass, chairs, even a file cabinet.

Within minutes of arrival, bodies of several people landed near the rig, only recognizable as bone, tissue, and blood after the fall of over a hundred stories. At first, Spinard and Casaliggi jumped into the truck for shelter, then retreated to a guard booth in the middle of the street, which had reinforced glass.

Inside the lobby, everything was happening very quickly. People were coming down the stairs to exit the building. Fire units were rushing into the lobby to report to Chief Hayden and me for their assignments.

Then we heard another loud, low-flying commercial airliner bearing down on lower Manhattan, this time approaching the World Trade Center from the direction of the Statue of Liberty.

4

DÉJÀ VU

T HE DEAFENING WHINE OF jet engines suddenly filled the lobby of the North Tower, ten times louder than the noise I had heard on the street. It sounded like a jet fighter on a low-flying attack. We all froze, then heard an explosion like the detonation of a massive bomb. The North Tower shuddered. Through the tall lobby windows above the mezzanine, I saw flaming debris rain down outside.

It was 9:03 a.m.

I heard Joe Casaliggi of Engine 7 as he reentered the building.

"There were two planes," he said. "I just saw the second one hit the other tower."

A second plane had hit the South Tower. Our problems had just doubled. In seventeen minutes, we had two 110-story buildings struck by commercial airliners, leaving multistory gaping holes and triggering infernos. Though I had ordered the South Tower evacuated, I had no idea how many people had gotten out. Fires raged above, though we weren't sure at the time on which floors.

At this point, we had no doubt that this was terrorism. I wondered if there would be other attacks. How bad was it going to get? While this was in the back of my mind, I had to focus on the firefighters we were sending up into the North Tower. The chief of department and other high-ranking chiefs would consider these other possibilities.

As I was trying to process this second attack, Assistant Chiefs Donald Burns and Joseph Callan entered the North Tower lobby. Chief Burns was the most experienced chief on the job. I'd known Chief Callan for years; he'd been an instructor for a prep course I'd taken for the promotion test. The FDNY's most knowledgeable team of chiefs, with decades of experience, had arrived in the North Tower lobby to manage an intensifying and unprecedented crisis. We had to reorganize.

Callan had been walking around the exterior of the North Tower, trying to see how many floors were on fire, when the second plane hit. That was when he knew for sure it wasn't an accident. He immediately rushed to the lobby to take command.

Now he collected all of us chiefs in a football huddle.

"We got to split our group," Chief Burns said. He'd take the South Tower command. Callan would command in the North Tower with Hayden, who immediately said, "I need Joe to stay with me."

"Okay, I'll take Orio with me," Burns said.

Before they moved to the other tower, we needed to coordinate our communications on a command channel. Orio and I stood several yards apart and tried to talk to each other over the repeater channel, but the system wasn't working properly. We decided it was safer to use the repeater in my chief's car. I asked Ed Fahey to turn it on and bring me the handie-talkie radio for that repeater. Chiefs would use channel 2 with my radio boosted by my car's repeater for command. Chiefs' aides, as well as all firefighters, would operate on channel 1 as the tactical, point-to-point communication channel. This was an established FDNY procedure at large fire scenes.

From the ICP on the far side of West Street, Chiefs Ganci and Cassano could oversee the two operations posts in each of the burning towers. Ganci also created a sector in the Marriott Hotel, which was between the two towers, and placed Deputy Chief Thomas Galvin in charge of evacuating the guests and employees. Ganci asked Assistant Chief Gerard Barbara to assemble units to be deployed to the South Tower for rescue operations. The ICP was intended to keep eyes on all three buildings from a safe distance.

A New York City executive order states that for a fire, sister agencies must report to the Incident Command Post established by the FDNY. This was the biggest NYC fire in a century. But the NYPD had set up a separate command post at Church and Vesey, more than a block and a half away, nowhere near the Fire Department's ICP.

Responding to the attack, NYPD Chief of Department Joseph Esposito ordered a level-four mobilization, the highest possible, which brought 1,000 police officers to the scene. After the second plane hit, he ordered a second level-four mobilization, bringing the total number of police officers to nearly 2,000. He also reiterated the order not to attempt any roof rescue by helicopters.

Some NYPD police officers from the Emergency Service Unit (ESU) came into the towers; most other officers stayed outside the buildings, setting up a perimeter to keep people safe from falling debris. They had a more robust radio system than ours, composed of hundreds of repeaters throughout the city. Their system allowed better communications in high-rise buildings and ensured no single point of failure. Police officers in helicopters could also communicate what they observed from above to those below.

By this time, FDNY chiefs had transmitted three fifth alarms and an additional second alarm, bringing almost one thousand firefighters and EMS personnel to the scene—over 250 units, about half of our on-duty force. The FDNY had staged more than a hundred ambulances a few blocks away, just northwest of West and Vesey Streets in Battery Park City.

INSIDE THE NORTH TOWER LOBBY, I heard a thunderous crash on the Plexiglas canopy over the entrance where my car was parked. Then came another sharp blow.

The distinctive thud sounds were human bodies hitting the canopy. As the fire raged out of control, people had begun leaping from the upper floors. Each unnerving crash was a life extinguished—and also a grave threat to first responders. At 9:30 a.m., a falling body crushed a firefighter as he reported to the South Tower, our first FDNY casualty.

The sickening sounds filled me with horror. I could only imagine how intensely the fire raged above if people had to make a gruesome choice between being burned to death or taking that leap. As the time between the falling bodies grew shorter and shorter, in a moment of frustration I grabbed the building's public-address microphone.

"Firefighters are coming to rescue you," I said. "Please hold on." I was hoping against hope that desperate people might hear my plea. Whether they heard it or not, my message did nothing to stop the terrible sound of bodies hitting the Plexiglas, about one jumper every couple of minutes just on the west side of the building. With great effort, we had to accept there was nothing we could do for these people in the moment and refocus on rescuing those we still could save. We positioned a firefighter outside to watch for falling bodies and warn new arrivals to look up before entering the building.

Fire Commissioner Thomas Von Essen and First Deputy Commissioner William Feehan, the civilian leadership of the FDNY, appeared at the command post in the North Lobby. The fire commissioner had been appointed by Mayor Rudy Giuliani to run the Fire Department, but had no role in commanding at fires. However, Feehan had been one of the most experienced and well-respected fire chiefs in the FDNY. (He was a former chief of department and fire commissioner.) Under Fire Commissioner Von Essen, he returned as the first deputy commissioner.

"You're not supposed to be here," Chief Hayden told Von Essen. "It's too dangerous."

And it wasn't Von Essen's job. Yes, the commissioner wanted to show his deep concern for those who were in danger. But his job was to be with the mayor to manage the city's response. We told him that our priority was to evacuate those below the impact zone, then attempt to reach those who were trapped.

Joe Casaliggi, of Engine 7, ran up to me in the lobby. He'd found the replacement air bottle he'd been searching for for his SCBA. While outside with Spinard, he had radioed Captain Tardio. "Seven chauffeur doesn't have a radio," he said. "Should I stay with him or should I come back up with you? Do you need me?"

"Give Tommy your radio and come up," Casaliggi heard. But the communications channel was garbled. What Tardio had actually said was, "Don't give him your radio. Just come up to the 15th floor."

"Chief, I'm going up where Engine 7 is," Casaliggi said. "They're on the 15th floor. I don't have a radio."

I understood Casaliggi wanted to be with his unit, but no one could go up alone without a radio. It wasn't safe.

"If you don't have a radio," I told him, "you're not going anywhere without a partner."

Casaliggi waited in the lobby for a few minutes, then came up to me again. He wanted to do something useful.

"Chief, I'm sorry—I know you're busy," he said. "But if you're not sending me up, I'm gonna go back outside with Tommy and help him by the rig." As chauffeur, Spinard was to remain with Engine 7.

I said, "Fine, you go do that."

The situation immediately outside the building was growing more dangerous by the minute. Spinard's rig was getting pelted with debris; small bits of falling glass were punching holes in the hose pumping water from the hydrant to the building's standpipe system. That could reduce our water pressure and diminish our firefighting capability if it got worse.

Firefighters were arriving in the lobby from all five boroughs of New York City. We continued to send up more teams under the close supervision of battalion chiefs. On the way up, firefighters encouraged people they encountered going down to "keep going, don't stop, don't rest."

Descending stairs is easier than going up. Average folks who were uninjured could get down a flight of stairs in thirty to sixty seconds. A person on the 80th floor might take an hour to get down, depending on their stamina.

I saw office workers and visitors emerging in a steady flow from the stairwells onto the mezzanine level, where they were directed to exits. They looked concerned and worried. But nobody was running. They moved in groups at a steady pace, determined to get out. As the lines grew thinner, I knew we were making progress.

But circumstances were getting worse on the upper floors. Fueled by oxygen and combustible material, fire typically doubles every ninety seconds. As heat and smoke increase, fire can create a raging inferno hot enough to twist steel. This monster fire sought air from broken windows, burning everything in its path. Toxic black smoke filled the upper floors. We just didn't know which ones. Could we climb as high as the 90th floor before we encountered flames?

And how would the fire affect the integrity of the building?

The consensus from the senior chiefs was that an upper floor might eventually suffer a partial collapse due to the high temperature of the fire. If there was a collapse, it would probably be localized, over the space of a couple of hours. But I heard no one ever mention the possibility of a total sudden collapse of the building, nor was there any history of it.

I exchanged endless radio messages with firefighters on conditions they confronted as they continued the long climb up the stairwells of the North Tower. However, so far, no one had even smelled smoke in the stairwells.

At this point, I believed that we would be able to evacuate everyone below the fire. We had the bravest firefighters in the world. We had safety chiefs. We'd get as many people as possible out of the building; then we would fight the fire, floor by floor, to look for victims who might be alive but injured or trapped.

Once we found everyone we could reach, then we'd get out of the building and let the fire burn itself out. We had no other choice.

In a lull between sending firefighters up, I saw Father Mychal Judge standing in the lobby, hands behind his back, staring up at the floors above.

At large fires or emergencies, an FDNY chaplain is assigned to do pastoral care of first responders and the public. We often saw Father Judge, one of our favorite chaplains, at large fires. Wearing his white helmet with the rank of a deputy chief, a turnout coat, and a priest's white collar, he typically stood to the side within view of the command post.

For me, he was a reassuring sight at fires. Father Judge understood firefighters, the dangers, their struggles, their needs. Whenever called upon, he'd speak with sincere empathy and spirituality. More than any other person, sixty-eight-year-old Father Judge was the soul of the FDNY, offering care and compassion to firefighters in hospitals, burn units, and at wakes and funerals. I knew how much his presence meant to firefighters putting their lives on the line. At a fire scene, I would glance his way, and he would give me a nod that we were doing okay. When I saw his Irish smile, I knew everything would be fine.

But as he watched events unfold in the lobby of the North Tower, Father Judge looked at me with intense concern. He turned away, eyes downcast, pacing, lips moving in prayer. It was as if he stood in the Garden of Gethsemane, praying as Jesus did before his crucifixion, with all his strength. Physical prayer, asking God to intercede, for this terrible event to pass. I imagined he'd never prayed so hard in his life.

Unsettled, I turned my focus back to the radio. Father Judge had attended hundreds of big fires and always wore a smile. His grim face, etched with fear and worry for his flock, was a bad omen.

WHEN CASALIGGI DECIDED to rejoin Spinard, of Engine 7, he had to wait for a safe period between jumpers. But bodies were falling so frequently, he finally just ran.

When a body landed two feet from the pump panel, they knew they couldn't stay there. Taking shelter under the pedestrian footbridge that connected Three World Financial Center to the North Tower, Casaliggi and Spinard watched as glass panels on upper floors spun out of their fittings and exploded on the way down, as dozens of people jumped from the upper floors to their deaths.

At first, Casaliggi consoled himself with the belief that the bodies falling were people who had died on the plane's impact. Then he saw a man flapping his arms on the way down. The horrific realization that the fires were so intense that the best alternative was to jump made him feel helpless, one of the worst feelings for a firefighter. But there was nothing he could do—he could no longer safely enter the building.

5

———

A LOUD RUMBLING SOUND

While maintaining contact with firefighters in the North Tower, I kept trying to reach my counterpart Orio Palmer to learn what he was encountering in the South Tower. At times, I could hear him—the South Tower's repeater must have been working—but he could not hear my responses.

Palmer had found a working elevator in the South Tower. He had taken it to the 41st floor and began climbing the stairs to help people trapped on upper floors. Lieutenant Joe Leavey of Ladder 15—my South Street firehouse, part of Battalion 1—was heading up to help get them out.

In the North Tower, I was receiving reports from firefighters explaining situations confronting them on the long climb up the tower, but at times so many people were talking at once it was hard to understand them.

At 9:32 a.m., someone in the lobby yelled, "We have another plane coming in!"

A third plane? I immediately turned around and asked, "Who said that?" No one answered.

For Assistant Chief Callan, the highest-ranking chief in the North Tower, the possibility of another aircraft hitting the World Trade Center was too much. He instinctively depressed his radio button and said, "Car 4-David to all units, come down to the lobby, everyone down to the lobby now."

Firefighters were somewhere between the 2nd and 20th floors. For those close to the lobby, there was a good chance that at least some of the firefighters would have heard the message, yet none returned to the lobby.

The firefighters did not recognize "Car 4-David." Callan had unconsciously used his call number instead of the phrase "Command to all units," which would have alerted all the firefighters that he was talking to them. Without such context, it made no sense to abandon rescue operations.

Furthermore, the message was not repeated because we were unable to confirm the report of a third plane. The person who'd shouted it had left the building. After the threat of a third plane dissipated, the order to come down was abandoned.

As ENGINE 7 CLIMBED TOWARD the 70th floor in the North Tower, the interior of the stairwell grew warm. There were no windows or air current. Add the heat to the weight they were carrying and their stifling bunker gear.

"The adrenaline was pumping, your heart was pumping outta your chest," Captain Tardio said. On the 10th floor, they stopped to rest. Tardio insisted to his firefighters that they stick together. "Because if the shit hits the fan, I don't want to have to go looking for anybody. Okay? If we have to get out, if we're all together, we'll get out."

As Zoda climbed, he wondered what they were going to do when they got to the upper-floor staging area. "Will we be able to knock down the fire?"

I looked at the clock and estimated that we were nearly an hour into the incident and the first firefighters I had sent up had made it to around the 35th floor, some even farther. The crowded stream of people exiting the stairwells onto the mezzanine had slowed to a trickle. The able-bodied were assisting disabled people or those with injuries, slowing their own evacuation to save friends, even people they didn't know.

Suddenly, an elevator door opened into the lobby. Five men and three women stumbled out, gripping their belongings, staring at the apocalyptic sight that surrounded them. I had no idea how or why the door suddenly opened. They'd been stuck in the car since the first plane hit and had no idea how bad things were. They wasted no time leaving the building.

Chief of Rescue Ray Downey arrived. "We got three fifth alarms and it is chaos out there," Downey told me and Hayden. He said nobody should leave by the side of the tower closest to our command post to avoid being hit by the jumpers. As he left for the ICP on West Street, we received a radio message.

"Tower number 2, 19th floor, firefighter down," we heard. "Tower number 2, 19th floor, firefighter down." A firefighter going up the stairs in one of the towers was having chest pains. There was some confusion as to what tower he was in.

Firefighter Chris Waugh turned to me. "This is Tower 1?"

"This is Tower 1," I told him. Firefighters were coming into the

North Tower, even if they'd been ordered to report to the South. They didn't know the difference between Tower 1 and Tower 2, and dispatchers hadn't made it clear. The South Tower chiefs were frustrated because they didn't have the manpower they needed. I handed Waugh a black marker. "Put a big one here."

Waugh scribbled "Tower 1" on the marble top of the fire command station.

Thirty seconds later, at 9:59 a.m., I heard a strange rumbling sound. I had one or two seconds to decide what to do.

Intuitively I knew we had to move, and pushed people, including Ed Fahey and Jules, about fifteen feet toward a small alcove on our left. The rumble grew to a roar, as if we were standing underneath a trestle as a train passed overhead—a sound I will never forget. I suspected pieces of the plane or debris were falling from above and crashing through the glass windows or the elevator shaft. I thought those of us in the lobby were the ones in trouble.

The monster locomotive sound chased us until we reached a non-working escalator. A rush of debris and dust hit us from behind. I automatically crouched down, trying to make myself smaller before the inevitable impact.

But the terrifying sound passed. Then silence. Blackness. I couldn't see my hand in front of my face. The event—whatever it was—had taken all of nine seconds.

"Is everyone okay?" Chief Callan asked.

People coughed. Then Jules spoke: "Yeah, I'm okay."

Other people spoke up, saying they were all right.

"We have to get out of here," Callan said.

I knew the way out, so I remained calm. The air was so saturated with dust my lungs couldn't draw a clean breath. Jules turned on the light on top of his camera, which illuminated the floor, but the area was still pitch black.

I wasn't sure exactly what had happened, but one thing was clear: we couldn't command under these circumstances. I deliberately forced myself to think. If we in the lobby had to leave the North Tower, I had to pull our firefighters out of the building and regroup outside. With so many civilians still in the building, this was not an easy decision, but I knew it was the right thing to do. I turned to Hayden.

"I am going to evacuate the firefighters," I said. He nodded in agreement.

Never in the history of the FDNY had chiefs made the decision to abandon a burning building with over a thousand people in it. I grabbed the microphone of my portable radio:

"Command Post to Tower 1, all units evacuate the building." I repeated the order several times.

On the radio, I heard my message being relayed up to chiefs and fire units.

Even though I knew some firefighters heard my order to evacuate and were relaying my message to others, they were already dozens of floors above ground level—some possibly as high as the 50th floor, based on radio communications—and it would take time to get out.

ENGINE 7 WAS TAKING A breather in the hallway when the building had started to shake, swaying from side to side. Captain Tardio yelled at his men to get into the stairwell for safety. For nine seconds, they felt the building rock. Then it stopped.

They had no idea what had happened.

"All right, we can deal with that," someone said.

On the 19th floor, Walsh's Ladder 1 had gotten antsy. Searching the floors for victims had slowed them down. The men started to rejoin the climb when the building began to shake and shudder, flinging people against the walls and furniture. Lieutenant Walsh felt as if he were standing in a speeding subway car making abrupt turns. Like Engine 7, they dove into the staircase for protection and stood there for nine terrifying seconds as the walls danced and swayed. Dust and debris filtered into the stairwell.

The quake sent a shock wave of fear through O'Neill. "This is not a good situation," O'Neill told the guys. The radio traffic faded. "We're in trouble here. We're on our own now."

Seeing everyone shaken up unnerved Van Cleaf. Usually, in tough situations, more experienced firefighters would reassure him. "Because you depend on each other," Van Cleaf said. "But when you have eight or nine men in a hallway and you all have the same look, that just tells you that something's not right. Because never is everyone scared."

Lieutenant Walsh refocused the group. "Let's move on," he said. But no sooner did they start climbing the stairs again than they heard me give the order to get out of the building.

"When I heard the chief's voice, I knew it was time to leave," Walsh said. He radioed to Olsen, of Ladder 1, to get out, but the firefighter, who had reached the 22nd floor, didn't acknowledge hearing the command.

Ladder 1 had a long walk down. They abandoned their tools, but kept their flashlights and SCBAs. They thought they'd get out of the building, meet up with the chiefs, who would come up with a plan, and they'd go back in.

At first some firefighters were yelling to get out. Walsh tried to calm people down. They'd make it out just as fast in an orderly fashion. But other firefighters were far too unconcerned.

"I can remember a firefighter resting on the landing and I told them, 'We've heard to get out of the building,'" Walsh said. "A lot of them didn't have a sense of urgency, but the firefighters of Ladder 1 did."

"You start to feel your anxiety build up," Van Cleaf said. "You take a deep breath, and you say, It's going to be all right, let's just keep going. Brothers ahead of me, brothers behind me, we're in this together, we're fighting together, and we're going to do what we have to do."

At some point, Van Cleaf started to run. "I don't even know if I was touching stairs on my way down. When I got about to three or two is when I started to think of my family—you know, I got to get out of here."

Tardio and Engine 7 had made it up to the 30th floor when they encountered a chief, who had heard the command post evacuation order, running down the stairs. "All right, guys, we're getting out," he told Tardio and his firefighters. "Everybody, out of the building."

With over twenty years on the job, Tardio knew that when a chief said to leave, they were leaving. No questions asked. Tardio told the men to drop their hose, anything that would slow them down.

DOWNSTAIRS, THE LOBBY ALCOVE WAS still pitch black. Even so, I was confident I could lead others to the way out. Trying to get my bearings in the darkness, I felt something at my feet. I grabbed a flashlight from Fahey and bent down to see what it was.

The light from the flashlight and Jules's camera revealed our chaplain, Father Judge, on his back near the base of the escalators. His helmet had been knocked off and he lay motionless, face up, but he had no obvious injuries. I knelt by his side, removed his white Roman collar, opened his shirt, and checked for breathing and a pulse on his carotid artery. When I found none, I realized our kind and faithful chaplain was gone. I guessed that he'd had a heart attack. But the event had caused more marble and glass and fixtures to fall. He might have suffered injuries I couldn't see in the blackness.

Father Judge's death was a terrible blow. I knew people had died in the airplanes and on upper floors, and I knew the firefighters going up were at risk, but Judge was our chaplain, a compassionate soul who'd put himself in danger, by choice, to provide solace. A rare form of heroism. I wondered how many more people would lose their lives.

Firefighters, like soldiers, do not leave our people behind. Chief Hayden, his aide Chris Waugh, and two firefighters picked up Father Judge's body. They started to carry him up the escalator to a narrow pedestrian bridge, over West Street, connecting the World Trade Center to the World Financial Center.

"Wait at the top of the escalator," I told them. "I'll see if the bridge is intact."

While Callan stood at the top of the escalator and issued another evacuation order, I took Jules, Ed, and an EMT to see if the bridge, about fifty yards long, was still a safe way out. It was strewn with broken glass and other rubble but intact, for now the best exit, safe from jumpers and falling glass. I radioed Hayden by our call names.

"Battalion 1 to Division 1 . . . Battalion 1 to Division 1 . . ."

Hayden didn't answer. I assumed it was because he was carrying Father Judge. But I had to go back to make sure he got out.

We walked back over the bridge again, to the North Tower, looking for the men bearing the body of our beloved priest. But Hayden, and those carrying Father Judge, were gone.

I looked out a window and saw Hayden. Instead of waiting, they'd found another way out, which happened to be more dangerous, through the plaza. They handed Father Judge over to EMTs, who carried him a few blocks to St. Peter's Church, one of the oldest churches in New York, founded in 1785. They laid our chaplain's body in his bunker gear on the altar.

Relieved Hayden and the others were safe, for the third time my small crew and I crossed back over the pedestrian bridge, using up valuable minutes. It was about 10:20 a.m. when we emerged by the World Financial Center at ground level under the bridge, where we were protected from falling debris. We saw the ICP had been abandoned. Nobody was there to give orders. Nothing was on the radio but incomprehensible static. We were on our own.

UPSTAIRS, THE DESCENT CONTINUED. As Tardio and Engine 7 descended stairwell B, they ran into Captain Jay Jonas and members of Ladder 6, who were on a landing.

Jonas and his company had made it up to the 27th floor when the rumbling of the South Tower collapse prompted them to stop.

"All right, all right, we're going home," Jonas had said. "It's time for us to get out of here."

He'd thought to himself, "We're not going to make it out." But he didn't say that to his men.

On their way down, they'd found Josephine Harris, a fifty-nine-year-old bookkeeper for the Port Authority who worked on the 73rd floor. A few months earlier, Harris had been hit by an automobile and injured her back and leg. She had been released from the hospital the same day, able to walk with a brace, and returned to work. But she was still impaired. She had limped on her own down to the 20th or so floor before her legs gave out.

At this point, the firefighters from Ladder 6 were running for their lives. But it is not in the culture of the FDNY to leave a civilian to struggle alone, even at the risk of death.

"We'll bring her with us," Jonas said. He and the men of Ladder 6, who were still carrying all their tools, began helping her walk. But the going was so slow, they had to stand aside as faster-moving groups overtook them.

Tardio, who had been a firefighter in Ladder Company 6 and knew Jonas well, told them, "We gotta get out." Jonas nodded. They were going as fast as they could.

As Tardio and Engine 7 passed floors on their way down, their realization that they were in danger was steadily rising.

When they reached the lobby, the place that had been bustling an hour earlier resembled an abandoned combat zone, thick with debris and coated with gray dust. Tardio saw that the command board was still set up but the chiefs had vanished.

"Whoa, this is not a good sign," Captain Tardio said.

"It was unbelievable," said Pat Zoda. "Nobody was around. There was nobody at the command station. It looked like the end of the world."

ONCE OUTSIDE THE TOWER, I tried to get my bearings, to understand what had just happened. Looking across the street, I saw the Marriott Hotel had been heavily damaged. Amid a cloud of brownish-gray dust, single sheets of paper covered the road, as if a million office trash cans had been dumped.

I looked toward the South Tower, but all I could see was a cloud of dust and smoke, with bits of paper raining down like confetti. I assumed the smoke obscured the South Tower. But I couldn't make sense of the scene because of the damage and the dust. What had happened? How had all this dust been created? What had the rumbling been?

Jules, still with me, focused on documenting the destruction: destroyed vehicles, streets coated with gray powder, shell-shocked, dust-covered people staggering away from the WTC complex as if zombies in a movie about Armageddon.

I tried to figure out what to do next. There's always a next step. But I couldn't match what I saw to any previous experience. After a few minutes, I could not think my way out of this situation. Suddenly, for the second time that day, a cold chill ran down my spine. I had to trust my instincts; this was the wrong place to stand.

"We have to go," I firmly told those still with me. We walked swiftly north to the corner of West and Vesey Streets, for all practical purposes in front of the North Tower. We ran into Chief Cassano, who had been at the ICP with Ganci.

Cassano had been a lieutenant in Ladder 113 when I was a firefighter in Brooklyn. I used to get detailed to his firehouse since it was within my battalion. Warm and friendly, Cassano was one of my early mentors and someone I would work for through most of my career as a chief. Covered with dust, Cassano's face was distraught. Hayden appeared out of nowhere and the three of us briefly talked.

"Joe, move everyone to Chambers Street," Cassano said. Then he started to walk south with Hayden.

It was 10:28 a.m. As Cassano got the words out, the loud rumbling began again. The same terrible roar descended on us. Someone screamed, "The building is collapsing!"

I didn't look up. I ran down Vesey Street in the direction of the

Hudson River, chased by the rumbling sound. In heavy bunker gear, you can't run too fast or too far. I saw Jules running ahead of me. We made it only a little way before a gale of debris and dust overtook us. Jules ducked down between a TV news van and a car. Since my friend was in a T-shirt and I was wearing a helmet and bunker gear, I jumped on top of him and covered him with my turnout coat to protect him. But we were too close to the North Tower. We heard the noise of steel, glass, and concrete crashing all around us. We waited to be crushed.

6

CLOUD OF DARKNESS

THIS BEAUTIFUL SUMMER MORNING, so filled with bright sunshine, turned pitch black from the dust. In total darkness I bargained with God to see my family again. Then there was complete silence. It was like that muffled quiet after a first snowfall. For a couple of seconds, I wondered if I was still alive.

After a few moments, I stood up, covered head to toe in gray dust. I couldn't catch a breath of air without coughing. My eyes burned. I spat to clear my throat.

"Are you okay?" I asked Jules.

Jules struggled to his feet, realizing for the first time I was the one who had been on top of him. Except for scrapes and bruises, he was uninjured but also coated in gray gunk. His camera was apparently intact. He brushed debris from the lens and realized he was still filming.

"Okay," Jules said.

Suddenly, we heard a staccato *pop pop pop* from across the street—the unmistakable sound of gunfire.

"Get down! Get down!" I yelled to Jules. Again, we ducked behind a vehicle. I was afraid not only for myself, but for Jules. We had barely survived and now someone was shooting at us? Were there terrorists on the streets with guns?

A few moments passed. We again got to our feet. To our relief, we realized a police officer had shot out a plate-glass window in the office building across the street, trying to get inside to escape the suffocating dust.

"Okay, let's go now," I said.

Jules and I found a small coffee shop on Vesey Street where employees were handing out water bottles to firefighters, police, and anyone who needed it. Everyone was dazed; some were injured. I drank but had trouble clearing my throat.

The wind picked up and started to clear the air. Back out on the street, I looked toward the World Trade Center and saw a surreal mountain of destruction: twisted steel beams, pulverized concrete, smashed glass, and huge pockets of flame, all covered by a murky haze of smoke and dust.

For the first time, I realized that both towers had completely collapsed. The buildings were not hiding behind the smoke. They no longer existed. Though it was the second skyscraper to be hit, the South Tower had disintegrated first in fifty-six minutes, followed twenty-nine minutes later by the North Tower's collapse. As each Twin Tower pancaked from the top down, they destroyed everything beneath them, including the Marriott Hotel and surrounding buildings. Most of the sixteen-acre complex had been utterly demolished.

My mind reeled in disbelief. I tried to take it all in but could not. I had landed in a war zone. With fires burning everywhere, it looked like the whole world was on fire. The nightmare had unfolded in just 102 minutes, from the airplane hitting the North Tower at 8:46 a.m. to its collapse at 10:28 a.m.

Questions flooded my thoughts. How many people had we lost? I had sent a couple of hundred firefighters up those staircases. Had any of them survived? Where were my brother and Engine 33? Where were Engine 7 and Ladder 1? What about all the other units I'd ordered to evacuate?

Jules and I walked toward the burning piles of debris. Dozens of rigs had been destroyed. Dazed, injured people coated in powder staggered around like apparitions. First responders were on their knees, sifting through rubble. It looked, as Jules put it, like the "gateway to hell."

Jules was desperate to know what had happened to his brother. He believed Gédéon had gone up in the North Tower with Tony. They usually rode in Engine 7 together. It made sense that they'd come with us to the odor of gas call, though I didn't recall seeing either of them in the lobby. But I had been extraordinarily busy.

"I've got to find my brother," Jules said. "If you don't mind, I'm going home." Weary, coughing, crying, he began to walk back to the firehouse, asking every firefighter he saw, "Have you seen anyone from Engine 7 or Ladder 1?"

I knew Gédéon also would be worried about Jules. I thought of Kevin and the other firefighters I had told to go up stairwells—especially those from my firehouse—and then ordered to evacuate. Had they heard me? Where were Captain Tardio, Lieutenant Walsh, and their firefighters? They'd been among the first to go up inside the tower.

Heartsick, I pictured my brother's calm face as he headed toward his assignment. I fought to gain control of my fear and anxiety, to figure out what to do. Nothing I had ever experienced gave me any guidance. I had never felt so helpless.

I tried to call Kevin by radio, "Battalion 1 to Engine 33," and heard no answer. Radio traffic was cluttered, so it would not be unusual for him not to answer me. I assumed he would show up, and there was a lot to do.

. . .

AFTER HEARING MY ORDER to evacuate, the Duane Street firefighters had hit the lobby of the North Tower with minutes to spare.

Lieutenant Walsh and Ladder 1 briefly regrouped in the deserted lobby, amazed at the devastation. But they still had no idea the South Tower had collapsed. They started to exit the building through the broken windows. As Walsh walked under the overhang, he could hear and see bodies hitting the glass, others hitting the ground. On the corner of the building was a pile of bodies where people had been landing in the same spot.

Someone in the middle of the street yelled, "Wait, wait," throwing up his hands. Two people had jumped together. Olsen, who had rejoined the group, was too close and his bunker gear got spattered with blood. Walsh took a deep breath and ran about fifty yards to a pedestrian underpass, hoping nothing would hit him from above.

O'Neill was stunned to realize that Ladder 1's truck had been demolished by concrete and steel, but still didn't realize the South Tower had completely collapsed. He and Van Cleaf walked up West Street, followed by other members of their house. Someone came up to them to tell them they better move faster, that the North Tower was going to fall. The firefighters doubled their pace, difficult in bunker gear after their exhausting climb.

The group had made it about two blocks north on West Street when the terrible rumble began. The top of the North Tower came down, popping floor by floor as everyone below fled in panic, chased by the mushroom cloud of debris. O'Neill dropped his mask and took off, for the first time really and truly running flat-out for his life.

Lieutenant Walsh heard a tremendous roar and turned to look at the tower as it began to melt, starting high at the crash zone, "like a sandcastle in a rainstorm." Walsh dropped all his tools, shed his mask and helmet, and ran north, trying to outrace the roaring locomotive bearing down on him. He could hear steel beams hitting steel beams, "like an erector set breaking down." As the hot gale of dust and debris knocked him to the ground, he knew he was dead.

Eleven seconds later, he opened his eyes to blackness. He was covered in ash and could see little pockets of fire around him. "I thought I was in hell or purgatory at that point." Then Walsh realized he had survived.

After leaving the building, Olsen had sought refuge under a pedestrian walkway and run into Joey Angelini, a firefighter he knew from Rescue 1. They were facing each other when Olsen told him the building was "shivering and shaking" and he feared it was going to come down. No sooner did he get out the words than the building began to pancake. Both men took off running—Olsen ran north up toward Vesey Street, Joey went south toward Liberty Street. Olsen survived but his friend did not.

When Engine 7 firefighters exited the North Tower, Zoda thought the landscape around them looked "like the end of the world." The Marriott Hotel next door had been cut in half, crushed by the South Tower, which they still didn't realize had fallen.

Tardio told his firefighters to keep close and stay in front of him as they headed north on West Street. Then they heard the loud rumbling, looked up, and desperately tried to outrun the collapsing tower.

"It was like a landslide," Zoda said. "I was running and watching this cloud of smoke chasing me up West Street. And I said, I can't outrun this smoke."

Tardio was frozen in amazement for a moment or two before he started running, still carrying his mask and gear. Exhausted from climbing and descending thirty floors, he was caught by the tsunami of hot air and grit. He threw himself to the ground and covered up. He expected to be incinerated by a fireball.

Then it stopped. In the pitch black, Tardio got up on his knees. "Felt my hands. I had them." He took his first breath of air, like his face was "buried in sand." He swallowed dust but was finally able to get his mask on and breathe.

LIKE ME, firefighters who had managed to evacuate without serious injury started to move toward the vestiges of the World Trade Center they had barely escaped. Covered with dense gray dust, they looked like stone statues standing at the edge of the pile of twisted steel and crumbled concrete.

Their firefighter brothers were trapped beneath the twisted mayhem, maybe injured, dying. They started to pick their way across collapsed beams to search for survivors, only to retreat as material shifted beneath their feet, all too aware that voids might swallow them up.

"Mayday, mayday, mayday," my handie-talkie radio suddenly squawked loud and clear. It was the tactical channel. "Ladder 6 to Command, we are trapped on the 4th floor in the B stairs. Mayday, mayday, mayday."

With a rush of relief, I recognized the voice of Captain Jay Jonas, from Ladder 6, a firehouse in Chinatown. I had sent him and his unit up the B stairs early on. Jonas and at least a few others were alive. If they had lived, maybe Kevin had survived in a structural pocket and was awaiting rescue.

I had no idea how to find the B stairs of the North Tower in this vast mound of misshapen steel beams and concrete. One wrong step and I could be terribly injured.

I decided to try going in below street level, through WTC-6, an eight-story building, the shortest structure in the complex. Known as Custom House, it stood on Vesey Street. I knew a lower passageway from there into the North Tower, where I could access the B stairs in the basement.

I didn't know what I'd encounter, but I needed air. I'd left my SCBA in my vehicle, now crushed by tons of debris. I found another chief's car on the street, damaged but accessible. I borrowed a Halligan tool from a firefighter, popped the trunk of the vehicle, and found an SCBA. The masks, carried by all firefighters, not only provide air, but also emit a high-pitched alarm when the user stops breathing or remains immobile for more than thirty-five seconds. Firefighters can trigger the alarm if they are trapped.

WTC-6 had been damaged, but not completely destroyed. I asked a firefighter to go into the building with me, but it quickly became clear the destruction was so extensive, it was impossible to get through the passageway to the B stairwell. The twisted steel beams and pockets of fire made it too dangerous. I yelled for Jonas, listened for SCBA alarms, but heard nothing. The rescue would have to come from the top.

Back on the surface, wherever I walked, I saw no desks, no chairs, no computers, no phones. Everything was pulverized. Shredded paper— millions of pages of reports, financial documents, the detritus from hundreds of offices that had occupied the skyscrapers for decades—was inches deep.

The FDNY had to regroup, reorient, and rebuild a command structure. But how?

The sixteen-acre rubble field was divided roughly into four distinct sectors, essentially squares, with chunks of buildings blocking movement from sector to sector. Fires raged in adjacent buildings, particularly WTC-7.

We were not willing to jeopardize firefighters to go into a building that had been evacuated, but we couldn't let the fire jump the streets to other structures. However, the water main was broken.

Fresh firefighters, paramedics, EMTs, and doctors were arriving, eager to search for survivors, all asking, "How can I help?" People were digging ad hoc, a dangerous situation. We had fires raging throughout the complex and no water supply. We needed to reestablish command, but our upper ranks had been devastated, chiefs either missing or dead. The magnetic command board in the North Tower lobby—our only record of what units had been sent to which floors—had been destroyed.

Firefighters began organizing themselves from the bottom up instead of the top down, watching each other to make sure their buddies didn't slip into a void. The dust on the steel beams was as slippery as baby powder.

Little by little, I heard chiefs reporting in on the radio. Deputy Chiefs Charlie Blaich and Tom Haring announced they were taking command of their geographical sectors.

Chief Hayden appeared out of nowhere. After carrying Father Judge, he had been on West Street looking for the ICP when the North Tower began to collapse. Too close to outrun it, he and Sal Cassano had crawled under different rigs parked on the street to escape the onslaught. The vehicles were damaged, but they survived. Cassano had injured his back and had been taken to the hospital for treatment.

Hayden surveyed the chaos. Nobody knew where Ganci was, or even if he was alive. People needed direction. Hayden had to impose order, but how? He climbed up on a burned-out rig in roughly the middle of the rubble. He asked everyone to stop whatever they were doing and look at him.

Dozens of firefighters obeyed, turning to watch Hayden, covered in gray dust, standing atop the crumpled fire truck. Then he asked us to do something unusual.

"Take off your helmets," Chief Hayden said, "and we are going to have a moment of silence, because we lost a lot of people today."

Our helmets bear our rank, unit number, and soot from every fire we have ever fought. Our helmets are our identity. Firefighters don't take off their helmets for anybody. Hayden knew that. Nobody moved to comply.

"No, no, no," Hayden said. "Take off your helmets because we lost a lot of people and we'll have a moment of silence."

So, wherever we were standing in the vast debris field, members of the FDNY took off our helmets and bowed our heads in silence, as did Chief Hayden.

With that simple, ordinary gesture, Hayden brought us together. At that moment, we felt solidarity with each other in our human frailty. Our vision of being superhero firefighters, the often felt but unspoken motivation that prompted many of us to join the FDNY, had ended. We were only ordinary people.

"Okay, put on your helmets," Chief Hayden said, as he slapped his own helmet back on his head. He told everyone, whether on duty or off, to give officers their name, their unit, so they could keep track of them and their given assignments. "We have much work to do."

In the quiet moment of silence, he established command.

7

BROTHER SEARCHING
FOR BROTHER

THOUGH JULES BELIEVED HIS BROTHER had gone up in the North Tower with the probie, Gédéon and Tony had stayed behind in the firehouse. Tony had gone off duty and was about to leave. Then, suddenly, someone from the neighborhood pounded on the door of the firehouse and told them, "Excuse me. A plane just hit the World Trade Center."

Gédéon grabbed his camera, and the two went out on Church Street. Filming the North Tower burning and the reactions of those on the sidewalk, Gédéon immediately felt guilty. All summer long, he had wished for a big fire.

Then he felt a rush of fear. He knew that everyone from the Duane Street firehouse who had been on the odor of gas call would be responding—including Jules—and started to worry.

He and Tony returned to the firehouse. The firehouse housewatch computer started spitting out message after message calling for more units. Over the next twenty minutes, firefighters began arriving from home to grab their bunker gear and tools. But they had no rigs and no orders to report to the WTC. They began turning the Duane Street firehouse into an emergency triage center for injured civilians and firefighters who were sure to arrive, bringing out all the EMS equipment, blankets, and other supplies. A couple of doctors who worked across the street knocked on the door, volunteering to provide medical treatment.

Gédéon and Tony monitored the computer. Gédéon felt torn. He was responsible for putting Jules in danger. The film had been his idea; he was supposed to stick to their plan, to keep filming Tony, but he had to find Jules.

He again grabbed his camera and started slowly walking south on Church Street toward the WTC, taping people on the sidewalks, their shocked faces staring up as ambulances and fire trucks raced past. Periodically, he tilted the camera from the people to the burning skyscraper.

"I'm thinking, 'My God, this is too big,'" Gédéon said. "For two months, we're waiting for a fire, and all of a sudden the most incredible catastrophe is in front of you. And you think you're not ready." But the scene was too important not to document. He kept going.

Gédéon had pushed Jules into learning to film. Now, as he walked toward the burning WTC tower, Gédéon felt his passion to get the film made had put his brother's life in extreme danger.

The sidewalks grew crowded, chaotic, filled with people who had seen the plane hit, telling strangers what little they knew. He filmed their astonishment, their eyes saying, *This is not happening.*

Because lower Manhattan is a magnet for people from all over the world, they were speaking multiple languages, but the reaction was the same. Disbelief, shock, fear. Some were crying, in anguish for those they knew were trapped in the tower, for those who were jumping. It was as if the globe were under attack, not just a skyscraper in New York.

Three minutes after 9 a.m., Gédéon caught the fireball at the moment when the second aircraft slammed into the South Tower. Debris rained down onto the street, sending panicked people running. Black and white smoke from both towers churned into the blue sky. Shredded paper fluttered through the air toward the East River.

"It's like something out of *The Towering Inferno*, like a movie," one man told him, clinging to a street post and looking up at the buildings.

On Church Street, Gédéon filmed a smoking chunk of jet engine that had crashed through one of the buildings and landed on the sidewalk, as a police officer shooed the curious away.

"Clear this area, please," the cop told rubberneckers. "Please stay away. Whoa, what are you doing? This is evidence, you don't kick it. Just get away from the area. Just go."

Gédéon couldn't get closer to the trade center without a firefighter. More afraid for his brother than ever, he retraced his steps to the firehouse, hoping to get someone to bring him back to the site.

Tony ached to go to the WTC, to join in the biggest rescue operation any of the firefighters had ever seen, only to be told to stay put, to answer the phones. He watched TV in frustration, furious when he saw a report that a third terrorist plane had hit the Pentagon. Tony said, "The Pentagon's on fucking fire? War. This is war." He started to put on his boots.

Watching Tony get angry, swearing at the unknown perpetrators, Gédéon realized he was expressing what everyone felt. "I saw the firefighter in him taking over."

But without permission, Tony couldn't join Engine 7 and Ladder 1.

FIREFIGHTERS AND OTHER FDNY PERSONNEL were reporting to the scene, including Dr. Kerry Kelly, the chief medical officer whom I would come to know well. She had been at work seeing patients on Staten Island when the first plane hit the North Tower. Her job with the FDNY was to go to the command post at fire scenes and direct immediate treatment for injured firefighters.

Dr. Kelly parked her new department vehicle near the WTC about 9:30 a.m. Then she saw a molten car, which had been destroyed by jet fuel. She went from thinking "great parking spot" to "oh my goodness."

She put on her turnout coat over her dress. Realizing she had no helmet, she went to Ten House to borrow one. At the firehouse, she saw a TV report that the U.S. had been attacked. But by whom? Nothing made sense.

Back out on the street, the landscape around the WTC was littered with human remains.

"It was as though you were walking by an anatomy class of body parts," Dr. Kelly said. Above, she saw people leaping to their deaths. "It was awful and almost surreal at that time."

She rushed to the aid of firefighter Danny Suhr, whose skull had been crushed by a jumper when he reported to the South Tower. An ambulance took him to the hospital, but Suhr later died.

Dr. Kelly worked with Dr. David Prezant, another FDNY medical officer, to set up a triage area for people leaving the South Tower, which had been hit thirty minutes earlier by the second aircraft. Civilians with serious burns and other injuries poured into the street. The medics got them into ambulances, and when those were not available, started sending them to the waterfront to waiting boats.

MORE OFF-DUTY FIREFIGHTERS started arriving at the Duane Street firehouse, including former Battalion Chief Larry Byrnes, who had joined the Fire Department in 1957. Somewhat of a mentor to me, Byrnes was the one who insisted I take the most recent promotion test to deputy chief. Though he'd been retired three years, he joined the massive response being mounted by the FDNY.

"I couldn't wait," he said. "Because, you know what, they're my fire-fighters, it's my building, it's my city." He turned to Tony. "Get your gear all together. Get a flashlight, bottled water." Gédéon intended to go with them.

As Byrnes got into his bunker gear, he asked Gédéon to grab a box of medical gloves. Gédéon found the box and rushed back, but the retired chief and Tony had already departed, walking south on foot. Able to hear Tony talking on a wireless mic, he followed with his camera. But they got lost in the stream of humanity going north. Gédéon was furious at himself for losing his chance to get to Jules. He turned back to Duane Street.

At the firehouse, Gédéon watched the South Tower collapse on television and began to grapple with the horrifying idea that everyone in the firehouse was dead, including Jules.

He hitched a ride in the bed of a pickup truck back to the WTC with Firefighters Steve Rogers, John McConnachie, and Kirk Pritchard, who had responded on their own initiative to the firehouse. Pritchard had been my aide the night before and got off duty early. Rogers had driven his red pickup from Staten Island after hearing of the attacks on his car radio. McConnachie had come to lower Manhattan for a dentist appointment, but after seeing the WTC burning, he'd rushed to the firehouse.

The guys in the pickup saw the mayor and the police commissioner walking north, away from the WTC, with a stream of sobbing and shell-shocked civilians. Everyone was covered with fine pulverized dust.

Rogers told the mayor to direct injured people to the triage center at the Duane Street firehouse, then slowly continued through the smoke and ash toward the WTC.

He parked the truck at the corner of Church and Vesey. The fire-fighters got out, grabbed their tools, and started walking toward what remained of the South Tower, directing injured civilians to EMS trucks parked on Church Street. As they continued walking, they checked rigs for tools and masks. Most had already been stripped by other firefighters who needed gear.

Gédéon followed, filming firefighters and ordinary people escorting or carrying the wounded to the ambulances. That was when Gédéon came face-to-face with imminent danger to himself for the first time. "Every single cell of your body is telling you, 'You should not be here.' The scenery was radically different. I mean, it was white powder everywhere. Just a few people here and there and this kind of silence."

Gédéon was walking past Engine 21, parked on the side of the street, when he froze. "In my heart, there is this image of Jules," he said. "I'm sure he needs me. But there is a kind of force field pulling me back, telling me not to leave this fire truck." He stood immobilized as the three firefighters kept going, disappearing into the dust cloud.

Four minutes later, Gédéon saw Rogers, McConnachie, and Pritchard running toward him, pursued by the collapsing North Tower. Gédéon jumped into the belly of Engine 21 and curled into a fetal position, joined a moment later by a passing FBI agent.

"Everything is falling down and falling hard. I could hear pieces of steel crashing," Gédéon said. The truck windows shattered. Gédéon waited for a huge chunk of the building to crush him, to end his life.

When the collapse ended, Gédéon heard no screaming, no radio, no sound at all. He couldn't breathe. In the dark choking dust, Gédéon made a vow. If Jules lived, he'd be a better brother.

The truck was covered with debris. He shouted for help. Slowly he climbed out of the fire engine. Gédéon saw a large man he had filmed earlier lying in the middle of the street, knocked down by falling chunks of the building. He stopped to help the injured man.

"Let's go, you can make it," Gédéon said, trying to get him to his feet. "You have to walk, sir. You have to walk." Gédéon and the FBI agent half carried, half walked the injured, semiconscious man to a safer place.

During their rush to escape, Pritchard had been hit in the back by falling debris and was loaded into an ambulance. Rogers and McConnachie continued working, setting up a tower ladder to rescue people trapped on upper floors of nearby buildings. For an hour or so, they tried to put out fires. But Rogers had cut his hand and had trouble breathing. He went to St. Vincent's for treatment.

As he wandered in the dust, Gédéon felt useless. "I knew there was nothing I could really do. I mean, I was not a fireman. But as a cameraman, yeah, there was something I could do and that was to document what was happening." Alone, grief-stricken, Gédéon started walking back to the firehouse, filming with trembling hands through a landscape that looked like nuclear winter.

HEADING NORTH WITH NO IDEA where he was going, Dennis Tardio, of Engine 7, found Pat Zoda and Jamal Braithwaite, but feared his chauffeur Tommy Spinard and firefighter Joe Casaliggi, who had been outside tending the rig, were dead.

Members of Engine 7 helped Tardio take off his turnout coat, mask, and helmet. They were joined by Lieutenant Bill Walsh, of Ladder 1, who told Tardio he would help look for the missing men of both companies.

In the dust and the chaos, they began finding each other. Walsh and John O'Neill connected and began walking back to the firehouse. They encountered firefighters and EMS going the other way, back to the WTC site to start rescue work.

"It reminded me of the minutemen, these people that day," Walsh said. "They were just helping out."

Before noon, a command post had been established on Chambers and West Streets by Chief Frank Cruthers, who responded from home. In all directions were piles of rubble. I carefully picked my way across the debris, searching for survivors.

Ninety-one FDNY vehicles had been destroyed on the streets surrounding the complex. I knew without question it would be the worst loss of life in FDNY history.

Everybody was poking through the ruins—even those in command ranks—unless they'd gone to the hospital. I saw Battalion Chief Bobby Turner searching underneath the bridge. I told him, "Be careful, Bob. Don't get yourself killed."

Everyone was searching, listening for sounds of "mayday" or the peeps of SCBA alarms. Some were extinguishing fires.

In the afternoon, I heard the heartening news of the miraculous survival of Captain Jay Jonas and Ladder 6, who I had been unable to locate.

Captain Jonas and the entire company of Ladder 6—Firefighters Bill Butler, Tom Falco, Mike Meldrum, Sal D'Agostino, and Matt Komorowski—had managed to carry Josephine Harris down to the 4th floor.

There, she quit. She could go no farther and urged them to leave her. Jonas refused. He tried to find a chair to carry her down, but couldn't find anything suitable and continued assisting her down the stairs. Then the building started to pancake, blasting air down the stairwell.

When the building collapsed, it formed a small pocket in the B stairs. About a dozen people descending the B stairwell had gotten trapped in black voids of jagged steel. Harris was battered and frightened but alive, thanks to the firefighters of Ladder 6, who'd surrounded her, also alive but trapped.

In a lower pocket near the 3rd floor was Richard Picciotto, a hard-charging Battalion 11 chief who knew Jonas well. He'd made it up to a floor in the mid-30s when the South Tower fell. He started yelling a command to evacuate by radio and bullhorn as he descended, telling people to get out with real urgency, which undoubtedly saved lives.

Unable to go down, the men talked to each other to share information and keep their spirits up while trying to figure out how to escape their claustrophobic, unstable catacomb. Many of them were injured. Battalion Chief Richard Prunty initially answered their roll call but died from his traumatic injuries before he could be rescued. There seemed to be no way out, but they began working to move rubble inside their precarious prison, talking only rarely to preserve their radios.

Jonas got a response from Deputy Chief Nick Visconti. At least they knew people were looking for them. Picciotto made contact with Mark Ferran, Chief of Battalion 12, who informed the shocked survivors that the entire building had collapsed. They were entombed in a mountain of rubble with no distinguishing landmarks. Even when Picciotto triggered the siren on his bullhorn, Ferran had no idea where the staircase was.

As fires raged in the rubble field, Ladder 43 searched for stairwell B and its small band of survivors, who grew more anxious as the minutes ticked away. By early afternoon, the black smoke and dust trapped in the voids began to settle. Sunlight from the outside penetrated their surroundings, literal rays of hope showing a glimpse of bright blue sky.

With the help from a spot of sunlight, Picciotto climbed up to Jonas.

They had to go up, not down, to escape. It was decided that Picciotto would go first. Ladder 6 tied him to their lifesaving rope for safety, in case he fell. When Picciotto got out, he tied the rope to a beam. Then some of the injured firefighters of Ladder 6 climbed out of the rubble.

When rescuers from Ladder 43 saw them, they couldn't believe it. Quickly Lieutenant Glenn Rohan from Ladder 43 led his firefighters into the collapsed stairwell. They followed the rope to get down to Jonas and the other firefighters from Ladder 6 who remained with Harris. Once Ladder 43 made contact with Harris, Captain Jonas took the rest of his unit up and out. The rescue operation required Harris to be carried out in a Stokes basket to safety. It was a remarkable tale of firefighters' strength, endurance, caring for others, and determination to survive.

Other searches were bearing fruit as well. Lieutenant Joe Torrillo, head of the FDNY's Fire Safety Education Unit, was buried in the South Tower collapse near the West Street pedestrian bridge. He had been found with a fractured skull, broken arm, and broken ribs.

Captain Al Fuentes of the Marine Division, who commanded Brooklyn's fireboats, had rushed to the WTC after the attack. He was pulled from the ruins alive about two hours after being struck by steel beams in the collapse of the North Tower. In a drug-induced coma for a week, Fuentes had suffered six broken ribs, a collapsed lung, and a skull fracture, and he'd needed several hundred stitches on his scalp, broken wrist, and fingers.

As I heard these remarkable stories, I hoped that Kevin had survived as well and was awaiting rescue.

I saw Engine 33 intact on the corner of West and Vesey. For some reason, I checked the officer's riding list of everyone working that day. I had to convince myself that I had really seen my brother that morning, that he really had gone up in the tower. Kevin's name was on top of the three-by-five card on the officer's dash. I thought, *Well, he'll find me.* I was wearing a white battalion chief helmet. There were far fewer chiefs with white helmets than the hundreds of firefighters wearing black helmets. It would be easier for him to see me before I saw him.

As chiefs took over sectors, they organized some units to fight fires that were burning everywhere. But the hydrant system and city mains in the vicinity of the WTC were compromised by the collapse of the towers. FDNY fireboats, along with the retired fireboat *John J. Harvey*, which had rushed down the river soon after the attacks, began drafting water from the Hudson River to fight fires on the west side of the complex.

Remarkably, a flotilla of citizens' watercraft began streaming toward lower Manhattan. Bridges, tunnels, and highways had been shut down, as had the airspace over the city. Hundreds of thousands of panicked people were trapped on the island with no way off. Ferries and boaters already on the water had come to their rescue and had quickly been overwhelmed.

Then the U.S. Coast Guard put out a call for help. Water taxis, tugs, party boats, fishing boats, vessels big and small streamed toward the docks and began evacuating people, taking as many as they could, dropping them off in Staten Island or New Jersey, then returning for more. An estimated 150 boats helped nearly a half million people get off the island, facing considerable risk since we had no idea if another attack was imminent. Their willingness to help was impressive.

GÉDÉON HAD RETURNED TO THE firehouse after his own near-death experience. As the hours passed, he asked each person trudging in from the WTC if they had news of Jules. No one had seen him since that morning in the North Tower lobby.

"Everyone's asking me, 'What happened, what happened?'" one firefighter told Gédéon. "I said, 'Hell is what happened.'"

"It just came down," said another. "And it wasn't supposed to come down."

As people continued to straggle in throughout the afternoon, Gédéon came to accept that Jules was dead. But he continued to ask. When a newly arrived firefighter approached him, Gédéon asked, "Have you see Jules?"

"Yes," the guy said. "He's behind you."

Gédéon turned to see Jules standing in the apparatus bay, his shoulders slumped in exhaustion and grief, his eyes red from debris and crying. The brothers embraced and wept as they tried to sort out what had happened to each of them since breakfast that morning. Jules told Gédéon, "I know now what it's like to think you're going to die."

A firefighter later went up to Jules and hugged him. "You know, yesterday you had one brother—today you have fifty."

As DAZED AND DUST-COVERED FIREFIGHTERS returned to the firehouse, they would hug each other with watery eyes, glad to be alive.

"It was like getting home," Walsh said. People that O'Neill thought didn't know his name were embracing him, saying, "John, I'm so glad you made it."

Tardio and several others stayed at the debris field. After getting their eyes washed out by EMS, they started digging, trying to find survivors.

But after searching through the afternoon, they'd found only one deceased civilian. They immediately set up a temporary morgue in the World Financial Center.

They made it back to the firehouse early in the evening. Firefighters were throwing up in the street, trying to purge themselves of the dust. Crying. Hugging each other.

Tardio learned that Casaliggi and Spinard had been injured in the fall of the South Tower. While being treated in an ambulance, they'd had to get out and run to escape the fall of the North Tower. Though they tried to radio Engine 7, they never got an answer. Casaliggi ended up at the hospital for treatment and was released in midafternoon. He'd believed everyone but he and the chauffeur were dead.

Spinard was "going nuts, thinking, Where's my guys?" He stayed in the rubble to look for survivors. He saw many body parts but only one or two whole bodies. Spinard, who had spent all 102 minutes of the event outside the buildings, developed breathing problems and would spend five weeks on medical leave.

I would return hours later, but Jules, who was back at the firehouse, told everyone that I had survived. Besides me, one of the last to return to the firehouse had been Tony Benetatos. The probie had worked with retired Chief Larry Byrnes to find survivors. Tony had seen chilling sights, including one man holding his right arm in his left hand as he ran screaming, "I need a medic! I got a bad bleed."

Tony was sent to lower the American flag at the firehouse to half-staff in honor of the many firefighters we'd lost that day.

THAT NIGHT, the firehouse ordered twenty pizzas. But it wasn't a party atmosphere. People talked about what they needed to do next. Some were already talking about going back to the site to join the search.

O'Neill told the guys they had to get back down to the site to find their truck. "I left my wallet on the dashboard," he said.

"The truck is crushed," Zoda told him. "I don't think you're getting your wallet back." Then he realized O'Neill was pulling his leg, something to bust the guys out of their daze.

The firehouse was dark, lit only by candlelight and partially by a generator. In silence, the firefighters listened to President George W. Bush on the radio. Everyone tried to make sense of what had happened that day, how they had been in the thick of it from the beginning but survived. It seemed statistically impossible.

It was a sobering thought, especially as the enormity of their losses was becoming apparent.

Tardio couldn't sleep. Eating an apple at about 4 a.m., he walked down to Church Street and looked south. The two 110-story buildings, such a prominent feature of his daily skyline, were gone.

"I can't believe they are not there anymore," Tardio said. "How did we make it out of that building? Thirty seconds, another two flights higher . . . Why am I alive and so many others are dead?"

It was a question that would plague many others for years to come.

"Yeah, I don't know why myself and the other guys were picked to survive this," said O'Neill. "In a way, I feel that there must be a reason. What am I supposed to do to earn this?"

I HAD TRIED TO CALL my wife, Ginny, several times that afternoon. I knew she would be out of her mind with worry. But I couldn't get through on either my battalion chief cell phone or a landline. Cell towers had lost power, or maybe millions of people were jamming the lines. In midafternoon, I finally borrowed another guy's cell phone, and, standing in the street to get a signal, I got a message through to my aunt Marie in Queens, my mother's sister who lived three houses from my parents. "I'm alive. I don't know where Kevin is. Please let Ginny know." I knew my aunt would spread the word to my parents, Ginny, and the entire family.

WITH WATER FROM THE RIVER now available, we could extinguish some of the fires. But the blazes in WTC-7 had grown. The sprinkler systems on the lower floors of the forty-seven-floor building were fed directly by the city mains and on the upper floors by a gravity tank with backup water from the city mains, which were inoperable.

Over the next couple of hours, we held serious discussions about the risks and feasibility of fighting the fires in WTC-7. Without water for the sprinkler system, we made the decision not to send firefighters into the building. The fires burned out of control.

By late afternoon, fire could be seen on multiple floors of WTC-7. The idea that a forty-seven-story building would be left to collapse would have seemed preposterous that morning. Now it almost seemed inevitable. A final order was given to abandon the building.

"It was just one of those wars we were going to lose," as Chief Peter Hayden put it.

I met up with Chief Daniel Nigro and Chief Frank Cruthers on the street at West and Vesey. I knew the building better than anyone. I told Nigro that there was a tank with 5,000 gallons of fuel for generators in the ceiling of the WTC-7 lobby. When the fire hit that, the result could be an explosion and the fire would increase. We needed to clear the area of people.

Just before 5 p.m., Nigro gave the order to pull the rescue teams back from the debris field around WTC-7.

Twenty minutes later, at 5:20 p.m., we watched as WTC-7 collapsed with that by now familiar roar, sending another cloud of gray debris and dust over the ruined landscape.

I WAITED FOR THE NEW dust cloud to settle. Having worked for twenty-four hours, I needed to rest for a couple of minutes before going back to search for my brother and other victims. I walked up Vesey Street toward the Hudson River and the North Cove Marina. My steps created little dust pillows that looked like powder snow.

I found an empty bench coated with dust and sat down facing the Hudson River. My face, mustache, and bunker gear were also coated in dust. I imagined I looked like a bizarre figure carved of gray marble.

I gazed into the distance, physically and mentally exhausted. I needed to think. How could skyscrapers just vanish into piles of twisted debris? Where's Kevin and other firefighters I ordered to evacuate? What do I, as a battalion chief, do now in this unthinkable disaster?

With every breath, I tasted the pulverized cement like a dry paste on my tongue. My eyes burned as I blinked, trying to focus with hundreds of specks in my eyes. After the dust from the collapse of WTC-7 had settled, I returned to the rubble field and continued to search for victims well into the evening, picking my way across steel beams and chunks of concrete. I listened for tapping or yelling or the high-pitched beeps of SCBA alarms. I heard nothing but other rescuers calling out.

Darkness fell about 7:30 p.m. Con Ed's electrical power grid in lower Manhattan had been destroyed. Some big searchlights running off generators were brought in; for the most part, we used flashlights to keep searching.

I continued to walk the site looking for my brother and survivors trapped by the rubble. Not only the Twin Towers but the entire complex of WTC buildings had been destroyed. The rubble field was immense.

I saw no one from Kevin's company, dead or alive, and a sick feeling coiled in the pit of my stomach.

By 11 p.m., I had been working for over twenty-nine hours, and awake for almost forty. The adrenaline rush of dealing with the crisis had long since ebbed. I hadn't eaten since 8 a.m. and could feel the stress and exhaustion slowing my reflexes, my thinking. I was afraid I was no longer helpful.

Coughing up dust, bone-weary, I began walking up West Street, zigzagging seven blocks back to the firehouse. I could barely see; in the heavy boots, my feet hurt so much all I could do was shuffle.

As I walked, an eerie gray dust cloud hung over lower Manhattan. I saw no one on the streets except other firefighters or police officers, moving like ghosts in the night. On the worst day of my life, I was profoundly alone.

The entire downtown Manhattan area had lost power. Thanks to a backup generator in the courtyard, in addition to candles, a few lights were on in the Duane Street firehouse. I could hear the TV as news reporters talked about a third plane hitting the Pentagon and a fourth crashing in a field in Pennsylvania. I couldn't grasp what they were saying. Were the four aircraft all connected? It seemed impossible, unimaginable.

After I dropped my dusty bunker gear in my locker, I asked if everyone was okay, afraid to hear the answer.

It was shocking.

Everyone from the Duane Street firehouse, all fifty-five firefighters and officers—the thirteen of us on duty and the forty-two who'd rushed to assist them—had survived.

Not a single person was missing or dead. All accounted for. Tardio,

Walsh, and the firefighters of Engine 7 and Ladder 1 who had answered the call with me that morning, who had gone up inside the North Tower first, had made it out. Some were injured, but they were all alive. Relief washed over me, but I didn't comprehend right away that it was a miracle.

In a state beyond exhaustion, body aching and eyes burning, I got into my car to go home. Lower Manhattan had no streetlights or traffic signals. Thankfully, no one else was on the road as I struggled to keep the car in one lane. I'd never seen the streets so empty. The horror had driven everyone in New York inside, huddling for protection, perhaps out of fear there'd be yet another attack.

Rainbow halos encircled the streetlights in Queens no matter how much I blinked to clear the grit from my eyes. I got to my home around midnight. I unlocked the front door and climbed the squeaking wooden stair to the bedrooms.

8

FEAR AT HOME

O N THE MORNING OF SEPTEMBER 11, Ginny had been at our home, sitting in our breakfast nook, drinking coffee and reading a book.

Ginny knew firefighting was a dangerous job; statistics show it is more dangerous than police work. But like every spouse of a firefighter, she pushed that reality to the back of her mind. I loved the FDNY, and she was secretly happy to have time alone when I was working a twenty-four-hour shift. She had some time to herself, to relax from the demands of her job as a nurse at the Memorial Sloan Kettering Cancer Center and her involvement with our children's schools and competitive swimming schedule.

We live in a very close-knit neighborhood with attached houses, and our neighbors are like family. A little before 9 a.m., our neighbor Reta waved at Ginny from her yard and said she should go down to the park and watch the fire at the World Trade Center.

"Joseph is working there today," Ginny told Reta. Instead of walking down to the park, she turned on the TV and saw the top of the North Tower engulfed in flames.

She knew I was assigned to Battalion 1 in lower Manhattan and would be the first chief to arrive at the WTC, since I was on duty. Ginny was not too concerned since I had twenty years of experience fighting big fires and I taught about high-rise fires to new chiefs at the academy.

But when the South Tower collapsed, she went numb.

"This can't be happening," she told herself. The nightmare Ginny never allowed into her thoughts erupted into anxiety. By the time the North Tower collapsed, she was in full-fledged panic. What if her husband of seventeen years didn't come home?

Was she a widow?

In her nursing career working with seriously ill patients, Ginny had learned to project outward calm so that patients and family members didn't get upset, and to focus on what she needed to do next. She did her best to marshal all that training now as she faced the loss not of a patient, but of her husband. Our children were safe at school, but she wanted them near, to hold them close. She tried to call the school, but couldn't get a dial tone. She finally got a call through to her older brother, Frank Schneider, a priest.

"Please help me, Frankie," she said through tears. "I don't know what to do. I know Joseph is there. I think he's dead."

Frank tried to reassure her. "Remember, Ginny, Joseph is very smart and he will figure out how to come home to you and the kids."

Ginny ran six blocks to St. Margaret's School, where Gregory was in eighth grade. She knew the principal, Sister Bridget, after years of giving hearing and eye tests to kids as a volunteer. Ginny knocked on the school door. When Sister Bridget answered, she explained that all the children had been gathered in the auditorium; many of the kids had parents who were firefighters, paramedics, or police officers. Ginny's determination to remain calm crumbled as she fell into the nun's arms, sobbing.

"I need to take Gregory home because I think my Joseph is gone. I know he is at the WTC. I don't know what to do." Sister Bridget held her as she cried.

Ginny and Greg walked back to our house. Christine was still in her high school class, five miles away. My wife and son sat on the sofa hugging each other, not knowing what to do or think. Hour after hour passed, and there was no message or call from me.

In the late afternoon, my father arrived. He and Ginny had always had a close relationship. A quiet, humble man, my father now looked to her "like a piece of him had been broken off."

"We heard from Joseph," he said. "He's okay, but we don't know where Kevin is."

She rejoiced to hear I was safe, but knew my father's heart was shattered at the thought his youngest child might not have survived.

About this time, a classmate's mother brought Chrissie home from high school. My wife and kids huddled together, knowing very little except that I was alive. She felt relief, but fears remained. Had I been injured? What about Kevin, her brother-in-law, our kids' favorite uncle?

That night, President George W. Bush appeared on television to speak to the nation. "Good evening. Today, our fellow citizens, our way of life, our very freedom came under attack in a series of deliberate and deadly terrorist acts."

For Ginny, it was much more personal than that.

We'd met when I was three months into firefighting. I had raised my right hand on September 5, 1981, and was sworn in to the FDNY in front of City Hall by then Mayor Ed Koch.

After the FDNY training academy, my first assignment was to Engine 234, a busy firehouse in Crown Heights, Brooklyn.

As a new firefighter, I cleaned the tools on the rig and the pots in the kitchen. My job was to learn from other firefighters, so I listened carefully to their fire stories and asked a lot of questions. I was curious to learn as much as I could from every fire and emergency. We were very busy, and I had at least an occupied structural fire or two every tour along with other small fires and emergencies. I was thrilled to be a firefighter, but considered it a temporary job.

I was in the middle of seminary, studying to be a Catholic priest. But I had requested a two-year leave of absence. I had applied to the FDNY four years earlier, while I was in college. I'd gone through a rigorous application process that included physical fitness evaluation and tests on fire department procedures and protocol. I had gotten high marks, but the job was so competitive, I hadn't been accepted until 1981.

I loved serving in various capacities in the community—prison and hospital ministry, working with folks in impoverished areas of New York. But once I heard I had been accepted by the FDNY, the adventure of being a firefighter was hard to resist. As much as I loved working with people, I wrestled with God over my vocation, over forgoing marriage, over the nature of good and evil and how I could make a difference when people are in need.

I figured I'd work as a firefighter for a couple of years, to enjoy the adventure, and return to seminary to finish my master's degree. Then I'd commit wholeheartedly to the priesthood.

After about three months of being a firefighter, my seminary classmates invited their families and me to attend their annual Christmas party, highlighted by the "end-of-semester skit," where they made fun of their professors. I was excited to return and see my friends.

The play was hilarious, and in the cafeteria later I caught up with classmates, assuring them I was coming back, but meanwhile having a ball as a firefighter.

One of my classmates, Frank Schneider, the play's director and an academic star, introduced me to his family, including his sister Ginny. We gazed at each other for a moment, and I wondered why I had never met her before. With dark brown hair down to her shoulders, hazel eyes, and a shy smile, she was cute and looked like a kind person. I could not keep my eyes off her and knew I wanted to get to know her better. I was twenty-five years old; she was a year younger and had an apartment in Manhattan. I was still living with my parents when I wasn't sleeping at the firehouse.

A couple of days later, I convinced Frank to give me his sister's phone number and to put in a word for me. I called her and left a message. Her brother told her to return the call. She finally did, and we made a dinner date.

We dined at a restaurant in Bay Ridge, an upscale area of Brooklyn, and fell in love.

The wrestling with God intensified. I drove Ginny crazy. She would ask, "Well, what do you do for a living?" "Oh, I fight fires, I save lives. Try to be a hero. But my life belongs to God." I guess I was caught up in the romance. She'd just laugh, knowing how much I loved her. Later, I told Ginny that she "stole me from the hand of God." The truth is that God had other plans for me. Better plans.

Every year, the St. Patrick's Day parade in March is a big deal for the FDNY. It stretches some thirty blocks up 5th Avenue from midtown to the Upper East Side. All the firehouses have people who march in the parade.

That year, since Ginny had an apartment on the Upper East Side, after the St. Paddy's Day parade, twenty firefighters crashed her place for a party. Ginny took the firefighters' bravado and jesting in stride and became a big hit with the guys.

We dated for a year and a half. At the end of what would have been my third year of seminary, my classmates were ordained deacons and made the commitment to celibacy. For me, it was Ginny and the FDNY, or the priesthood. I knew the answer in my heart was Ginny.

All that wrestling with God was over. I was in love with a beautiful and wonderful woman.

I proposed to Ginny and told the seminary I would not be returning. We got married on June 3, 1984. Her brother, now Father Frank Schneider, a diocesan priest, performed the ceremony. In fact, seventeen of my former classmates, now priests, concelebrated the wedding with us.

Living in Manhattan was very different from Queens. We went out to eat at least once a week, which was easier than cooking. All my spare time was spent studying FDNY manuals and building codes to earn a promotion to lieutenant. The FDNY was so competitive, 85 percent of people who took the test didn't make rank; if you failed, you wouldn't have a chance to retake it for four years. After my daughter was born, I rocked her crib with one foot while studying.

Ginny took my crazy schedule and constant studying in stride. As an oncology nurse, Ginny understood working under pressure. And together we worked out our schedule, with its emphasis on family, which was as important to her as it was to me. She had seven siblings. One sister married Richard Hogan, a firefighter she'd met through me. Rich's sister also married a firefighter, Hank Banker. Depending on our work schedules, three of us related by marriage might be on duty at the same time, in the same firehouse.

Ginny and her sister entered into the FDNY extended family with gusto. Like most FDNY firefighters and their spouses, we had an optimistic bias, even when a firefighter died in the line of duty. *That will never happen to us.*

Now, as Ginny watched TV on the night of September 11, her husband, brothers-in-law, firefighter friends, their wives and children—everyone in her extended family was under assault, facing unthinkable loss.

Kevin was a big part of her life as well as mine. He lived six blocks from our house, and half a block from our kids' school. Almost every day after school, the kids would stop by the three houses where he, my parents, and my aunt lived. They'd chat and get a snack. During the summer, Kevin would take the kids out on his sailboat or to play on the beach.

On the night of 9/11, emotionally exhausted, Ginny went to bed but was unable to sleep, tossing and turning as she wondered when she would see me again. When she heard the front door open and me walking up the creaky stairs of our seventy-two-year-old house, she rushed to the hallway at the top of the stairs to embrace me, weeping uncontrollably. Christine and Gregory burst from their rooms with cries of "Dad!" We hugged, cried, and desperately clung together, all of us drenched in tears of an emotional reunion, filled with love and disbelief.

Covered in light gray powder, with eyes so red they appeared to be bleeding, I must have looked like a ghost of myself. My body ached, and I could see in the mirror my face was filled with sadness. Ginny was overjoyed I had come home, yet she was afraid to hear any details of the horrors of the day. We climbed into bed and tried to sleep. I was never so happy to be home with my family and next to the woman I love.

9

THE PILE

MY EYES WERE OPEN BUT I couldn't see clearly. I blinked a few times and opened them again. Just a blur.

At midnight, after our emotional family reunion, I'd taken a shower and tumbled into bed. I could no longer move, not even to eat. I slept until 6 a.m. and awakened with eyes so puffy it pained me to open my lids. I had lived through 9/11, but now it was difficult to see.

I flashed back to childhood, when I was in second grade, just before Christmas, and woke up unable to see out of my left eye. It was swollen shut and painful. For a healthy kid who had never been sick enough to stay home from school, the situation was bizarre. Dr. John Scalzo, our family physician, came to my parents' house, examined me, and told them it was very serious; I needed to go to the hospital. I was immediately admitted. The next morning, I woke up and couldn't see out of my right eye.

Pediatric experts Dr. Eden and Dr. Kaufman were called in. They diagnosed a disease very rare in children: herpes zoster ophthalmicus, a shingles virus that could lead to permanent damage, even death. Blisters were forming over my eyes and it was progressing. In December 1963, my only hope was for doctors to push penicillin, delivered via a spinal tap. In twelve to twenty-four hours, they'd know if it had worked. Otherwise, I might die.

I could not be under sedation for the treatment and I was scared out of my mind. My parents were not allowed to be with me in the room. I knew I had to be courageous enough to listen to what I was being told, to be completely still. As Dr. Scalzo squeezed my hand, another inserted a needle into my spine. Despite the fear and pain, I didn't move.

The next morning, I woke up and I could see. After a week in the hospital, I spent several additional weeks with my face covered in hideous-smelling ointment. I recovered completely, the only evidence some scars on my forehead; eventually my treatment and recovery was written up in a medical journal. But that nightmarish childhood event traumatized my whole family.

As I blinked and thought about my parents' fear for their son's life, memories of the previous day's horrors at the WTC flooded back. I could feel the grit from the debris in my eyes; rinsing my eyes did nothing to alleviate the pain or clear up my sight. I called Dr. Tom Cunningham, my friend from grade school and college roommate, now a cardiologist.

"Tom, I can barely see."

Tom started crying. He'd seen the collapses on TV. Knowing I'd be in the thick of it, he had accepted that I had not survived. Thrilled to hear my voice, he hung up and arranged for me to see an eye doctor at 6:30 a.m. Ginny drove me to his office on the Queens–Nassau County border.

Dr. Willy Ky and Dr. Leslie Goldberg told me the grit from the collapse had worked its way under my eyelids, causing inflammation. I could only imagine what the grit was made of: pulverized glass, concrete, Sheetrock, and other toxic building materials. Dr. Ky removed fifty bits of debris, placed drops in my eyes, and told me to return to see him the next morning, when they'd take out fifty more pieces. That became my morning routine for the next three weeks, even on weekends.

After Dr. Ky's treatment, I could see well enough to drive to the Duane Street firehouse. Ginny understood when I insisted on going back to the site that morning instead of staying with her. "I have to find my brother and the other firefighters," I told her.

I arrived at about 8 a.m. Some firefighters had gone home to sleep for a few hours; others stayed the night. Grim-faced men sat around the kitchen table. A few watched TV news replaying the events of the previous day and the response of the U.S. authorities.

Belonging to a firehouse meant you had dozens of brothers and sometimes sisters, especially after many years in the department. Since the FDNY tends to run in families, many people had relatives and close friends who were missing. The joy of seeing people alive the previous night had given way to heartache.

The FDNY was just starting to grasp the size of our losses. Asked on television how many people had died, Mayor Giuliani shook his head and replied, "The number of deaths will be more than any of us can bear."

But New York wasn't alone in suffering. The previous night I had seen snatches of footage on the firehouse TV about an airplane hitting the Pentagon and another crashing in a field in Pennsylvania. None of it made sense to me. I would learn that terrorists with ties to a group called al-Qaeda had carried out four highly coordinated attacks. During his address to the nation, President Bush had said, "The United States will hunt down and punish those responsible for these cowardly acts."

American Airlines Flight 11, a Boeing 767 with ninety-two people aboard, had taken off from Boston's Logan Airport at 7:59 a.m., destination Los Angeles. Hijackers had overcome the crew, commandeered the cockpit, then flown the plane into floors 93 through 99 of the WTC North Tower at 8:46 a.m. From the street, I had witnessed the exact moment of impact, which had killed everyone on board and many inside. For the first time, I realized which floors had been destroyed by the aircraft. The flames had certainly spread to other floors as well.

United Airlines Flight 175, a Boeing 767 with sixty-five people aboard, had left Boston at 8:14 a.m., also headed to Los Angeles. It had crashed into floors 77 through 85 of the South Tower at 9:03 a.m., even as people evacuated. The damage was much lower down, meaning that those people above had little chance of getting out.

American Airlines Flight 77, a Boeing 757 with sixty-four people on board, had taken off at 8:20 a.m. from Dulles International Airport near Washington, D.C., headed to Los Angeles. The terrorists slammed it into the western walls of the Pentagon at 9:37 a.m. The casualties were much lower because it wasn't a high-rise building, but horrific nonetheless.

United Airlines Flight 93, a Boeing 757 with forty-four passengers, took off from Newark International Airport at 8:41 a.m., heading to San Francisco. The hijackers intended to crash it into the White House or the U.S. Capitol in Washington, D.C. As the crew and passengers fought to retake control, it crashed into a Pennsylvania field, near Shanksville, at 10:03 a.m. All of those brave people were killed.

I had trouble comprehending the staggering scale of the events that had occurred the previous day, and I had no time to watch TV or read the newspaper. Ginny sitting at home in Queens knew more about the big picture than I did.

By the time I arrived at the firehouse, the FDNY had gone to an emergency command structure. Some units would be assigned to WTC rescue operations, others to respond to emergencies in the rest of the city. To increase staff availability, firefighters would be working twenty-four hours on, twenty-four hours off until further notice.

Many of the guys with Engine 7 and Ladder 1 were anxious to get back to the WTC site to start searching; everyone assumed we had many people alive and trapped. I shared that feeling.

The previous day, Ron Schmutzler, the captain of Ladder 1, had left the firehouse at 8 a.m., took a train home, and was helping another firefighter with a chore when they heard the news on the radio. When the buildings collapsed on television, they started to cry, knowing the guys from their firehouse were in the middle of it.

"In my mind, they were all dead, there was no one going to survive something like this, and I knew I had to go in there and help," Schmutzler said. "I had to dig these guys out not knowing if there was going to be another collapse, another bomb, another explosion or whatever it was."

Schmutzler took the time to write a quick letter to his wife and kids, telling them he loved them, basically saying goodbye.

Then his son walked through the door. "There were tears in his eyes." Schmutzler hid the letter. The boy pleaded with him not to go back to work. The captain spent a few minutes talking to him about why he had to go. "If it was me in this collapse, I would be inside that building, alive, praying that my friends would come to rescue me. How would you feel if you found out that there were firefighters that stayed home when they should be in there rescuing me?"

"Then go," his son said. "But if you die I'll never forgive you."

"Well, I'm not going to die," Schmutzler had told him. "I'll be back." But he couldn't be sure.

The following day, Schmutzler knew how his men felt and wasn't going to hold them back from saving their brothers, even if it meant exposing themselves to danger. He announced that whoever wanted to go to the site could, and whoever was not yet up for it could hold off. "If you were ready to go down, you went down," Captain Schmutzler recalled. Otherwise, "you stayed in the firehouse and took care of the guys as they came back."

For those who went, there were rules. "Go in teams of two," Schmutzler told them. "One guy falls in a hole, we will have a guy there that knows you fell into that hole." Someone passed around extra surgical gloves for picking up body parts.

"Hey, guys," Schmutzler said as a group was getting ready to leave, "if you hear three horns it means something might be coming down, so keep your eyes open when you're walking around down there." Members of Ladder 1 started walking south to the site since their rig had been destroyed.

I put on my dusty bunker gear and started walking as well. My eyes were still scratchy and inflamed, but I could see. Nobody was on the street in lower Manhattan except emergency workers. Technically, I wasn't supposed to be on duty, but I had no thought of waiting to report until I was next scheduled to work. I had been first at the scene. In the FDNY, we take ownership. Sometimes, we name fires. In my mind, this was my fire. I knew other chiefs felt the same way.

I reached Ten House, directly across from the South Tower. At the corner of Liberty and Greenwich Streets, the firefighters of Ten House often kept the apparatus door open for neighbors and tourists. It had been damaged; the apparatus floor, where the rigs are normally parked, had been covered with debris, and the windows shattered. But for the most part it was usable. After most of the debris was removed, it became our new Incident Command Post and a place firefighters could get water or take a breather.

The previous day, searchers had found the bodies of Chief of Department Pete Ganci, Chief of Rescue Ray Downey, and First Deputy Commissioner William Feehan, who had walked south from the command post on West Street after the South Tower collapse. Chief Donald Burns and Chief Gerard Barbara also had been killed. Nineteen of twenty-three battalion chiefs, including Orio Palmer, had died. I was one of only four surviving battalion chiefs.

That our upper ranks had been devastated was very unusual. Chiefs don't go into burning buildings. Ganci was a hands-on guy, though. I suspected he'd wanted to direct the response to the collapse of the South Tower, got too close, and was caught by the second collapse. Daniel Nigro had immediately become chief of department.

The grayish-brown dust had settled a bit over the rubble field and, for the first time, I saw the massive aluminum and steel skeletons of the skyscrapers, with huge girders hanging precariously out of upper floors of adjacent buildings. At its tallest peak, the mountain of debris was perhaps six stories high. It was impossible to believe two 110-story buildings had once stood there. The extreme crush of the buildings' weight had pulverized everything.

Fires continued to blaze and smolder for the next four months. What we began calling "the Pile"—what the press would dub Ground Zero—was perceptibly heaving, settling, burning, exceedingly dangerous for any search and rescue operations. An acrid smell of burning fuel, concrete, plastic, and paper hung heavily in the air.

Volunteer rescuers—police officers, military personnel, and firefighters from around the world—wanted to help. But it was too dangerous for many folks who showed up. The National Guard was called to provide security; they cordoned off everything within blocks of the WTC complex because debris had fallen that far away.

That second day was a mad rush to search for any victims we could find without heavy equipment. An FDNY officer and five firefighters formed each of our rescue teams. Bucket brigades removed surface debris. Those sorting through the rubble listened for sounds of life; if anything was heard, they shouted, "Quiet!" Everybody stopped talking until the sound could be identified.

Smoke aggravated my eye injury, forcing me to stay off the rubble. But I could see people getting too close to unstable areas. I had to ask chiefs to help me literally push people out from under dangling steel beams. At times, the debris underfoot would shift and people retreated in haste, yelling, "Go, go, go!"

Some of the hazards weren't as obvious. Noxious air and dust prompted some people to start wearing medical masks. The fires gave off toxic fumes. We had shut off gas mains, but many of the buildings were heated by steam or diesel oil. What if an underground fire hit a diesel tank?

For nourishment that day, I had a bottle of water and a packet of four Oreo cookies from the Red Cross, which I put in a pocket of my turnout coat. That was lunch and dinner. Local restaurants began distributing meals to rescuers for free, but I was too busy to eat. I hoped my brother was alive somewhere under the mountain of rubble. We had to find him.

The day of grueling rescue efforts passed with few bright spots. At 9:15 that morning, a young woman who worked for the Port Authority had been pulled alive, though seriously injured, from the wreckage of the North Tower. That had given everybody hope. But when darkness fell, no additional survivors had been found.

The electrical power was still off in lower Manhattan. We brought in more emergency lighting for the second night. The beams illuminating the haze of dust over twisted steel and smashed concrete made the Pile seem like the set of an apocalyptic horror movie. We would keep looking through the night, but hope was fading fast.

When I started plodding back to the firehouse sometime after 8 p.m., my mind kept returning to my brother. He had gone up stairwell B. If he'd heard the order to retreat, he could have been in the vicinity of Captain Jay Jonas and his unit when the tower fell. Through some miracle, they had survived. Maybe Kevin had, too, and we just hadn't heard him yet.

I desperately wanted to believe that.

The tip of Manhattan was covered in haunting darkness, with only Ground Zero illuminated by floodlights reflecting off the dust cloud from the Pile. The roads were empty as I trudged up the middle of West Street to the firehouse. I tried to grasp the enormity of the last thirty-six hours.

I struggled with the reality that my brother Kevin could be dead. He'd followed me into the Rockaway Point Volunteer Fire Department and then the FDNY. He was my best friend and confidant, an adventurist who chose to live every day to the fullest. He knew me better than anyone.

I thought of the Pile. Each floor of the collapsed towers had been compressed into eighteen inches, with the immense weight of steel and concrete above. Even though we would keep searching, I knew there would be no more survivors.

My thoughts returned to my seminary days, when I grappled with deep theological issues of good and evil, then wrestled with God about my vocation in life: *Should I be a priest or get married?* A conversation I had had many times.

As I walked, I again began wrestling with God. How could anyone be so evil as to fly airplanes into buildings to kill innocent people? *What does all this mean? What do you want from me?* As I continued to slowly walk back to the firehouse, revisiting these questions felt like meeting an old friend on the road. My heart burned as I wondered what I was called to do. Strangely, there was comfort in knowing that I had been here before.

When I got to the firehouse, I felt the weight of the reality that Kevin was gone. I knew I had to go home to Queens and tell my parents. For the second night in a row, the drive home was not going to be easy.

10

AN AVALANCHE OF MEMORIES

I DIDN'T MINGLE WITH THE guys that night. With deep sadness, I drove to Queens. I still wore my uniform white shirt with gold oak leaves on the collar and an FDNY patch on the left arm, which made it easier to get through the checkpoints at street closings in lower Manhattan. Seeing military vehicles with a 50-caliber gun on top at each roadblock brought home the reality that we had been attacked.

Arriving on a quiet Queens block, I walked in the back door of my parents' small house, where I had grown up with my sister, Mary Ellen, one year younger than me, and Kevin. My parents greeted me with tears and hugs and questioning faces. They didn't want to ask me about Kevin, but I knew they had thought of nothing else all day.

We were a tight-knit family. My parents, Helen and Bill, had grown up in the same neighborhood, three blocks apart, in Queens. They both went to St. Margaret's Elementary School, the same school we three kids later attended as youngsters. After serving in the Navy as a signalman during World War II, my dad worked as a machinist before joining the U.S. Postal Service as a letter carrier. Mom had graduated from a secretarial high school, worked in New York City's controller's office, and then had a part-time job in a local clothing shop. They'd met after the war and he wooed her by writing a love poem: "One night a year ago, when there was lots of snow, I met you at a dance. It was the beginning of our romance . . ."

Family surrounded us. Nobody had much money. We thought we'd hit the jackpot because Dad was a letter carrier. Among factory workers, government jobs meant security. Or so we thought, until the post office went on strike.

My parents lived in a semidetached house that was no more than 600 square feet, with a postage-stamp yard. Eventually, we made the basement into two bedrooms. Two houses away lived my great-aunt Nell and uncle Tom, with my grandmother and my aunt Marie in a house right next to them. As kids, we ran between my aunt's and grandmother's houses through doors installed in the adjoining front porches. It seemed like one family.

Other family members lived close by, including my father's parents, who were three blocks away. My grandfather Nick, my mother's father, was a boisterous deputy sheriff in Queens County who sat at the head of the big table at Aunt Nell's at Thanksgiving and told stories about politics. I never saw him in uniform; when he died, I had to turn his gun in to the NYPD.

After school, we played stickball and handball in the streets, not to mention "ring-a-levio," a game where two groups of kids faced off against each other. A kid on one team would run and try to break through the other team's line of linked arms. As the older, bigger brother, I'd break through, but Kevin would get stuck. He was often frustrated trying to keep up with me, but away from the playground we were close. For most of my childhood, Kevin and I shared a room together. We'd talk all night, even though we were three years apart.

In the summers, we had no air-conditioning. To escape the heat, our family decamped to Breezy Point, the westernmost beach on the Rockaway peninsula, where my parents, with the help of my aunt and uncle, paid $3,000 to buy a summer bungalow, a small 500-square-foot fixer-upper. A modest beach community run by a cooperative, Breezy Point got its name from the winds off the Atlantic Ocean from the south and west, and the calmer waves on the north side, Jamaica Bay. It had few paved roads, just sand tracks, which kept development modest. If I walked a quarter mile, I'd hit the ocean; the other direction I'd hit the bay.

My parents, the three of us kids, my aunt and uncle, and other family members all slept in the tiny house on beds crammed into every corner. We spent our days walking on the beach, collecting shells, playing beach volleyball, swimming—and for my brother and me, handing tools to my father as he worked on the house. I learned how to paint, sand, saw, fix plumbing and electricity, helping whenever my dad needed another pair of hands. I would have preferred to play, but those skills later came in handy. It was also my daily job to rake shells and broken glass from the sand of our yard.

At the beach, I started swimming competitively. I'd win races; Kevin would try to copy me. In college, I got a job as an ocean lifeguard at Gateway National Recreation Area, at Jacob Riis Park. To escape the city's heat in the summer, residents crowded Riis Park until 10 p.m.

It was at Breezy Point that Kevin and I caught the bug that would prompt us to become firefighters.

The summer after I graduated from high school, my friend Peter Collins and I joined the Rockaway Point Volunteer Fire Department (RPVFD), the so-called "Vollies." I continued to lifeguard, but each Tuesday night we had drills and learned the basics of firefighting from the more senior volunteers, who called us the "snot-nosed kids."

Every summer during college and graduate school, I lived on Breezy Point with my parents, worked as a lifeguard, and responded to ambulance and fire calls when I was off. In the middle of the night, I'd hear the siren—one blast for an ambulance, three for a fire—throw on clothes, and sprint for the firehouse, about a quarter mile from my parents' house.

We had brush fires and a few blazes in the little wooden bungalows. We'd get a hose on the fire until FDNY firefighters arrived and took over. They had full jurisdiction but allowed the beach communities to have small volunteer departments because their big rigs couldn't run on the sand tracks.

Besides learning firefighting, I took first aid classes and was certified as an EMT, a certification I would keep for twenty-seven years. I even competed on the RPVFD First Aid team that went up against other ambulance corps in New York State, winning the state championship year after year.

With all that first aid knowledge, I went on more medical calls than fires. But no amount of training would prepare me for my worst ambulance call. In the middle of the afternoon, the siren sounded for an accident on Breezy Point: a little girl had been struck by an electric-utility van. I worked on her desperately to save her in the back of the ambulance as we swerved through traffic to the hospital. She didn't survive. The Vollies didn't have any counseling at the time. Not knowing what to do with the reality of her death, I just pushed it aside.

Kevin didn't become a lifeguard, but he did first aid on the beach. We ended up working in the same spot. Kevin also joined the Vollies as soon as he was old enough.

One year, after a hurricane, Kevin saw a damaged Hobie Cat in the surf off Riis Park. He swam out and pulled the eighteen-foot catamaran to shore. When the owner couldn't be located, the boat was going to be junked because the damage was too extensive for it to be sold. It would have cost a couple of thousand dollars to buy a new one, which we didn't have. So my brother repaired it.

My father thought we were crazy to take on major boat repairs, which required replacing almost all the rigging. But since he had served in the Navy in the South Pacific during the war, he secretly was proud of his sons, especially Kevin, who was motivated to tackle such a huge project.

Then we had to learn to sail. The Hobie Cat had two pontoons and a huge sail, and in certain conditions was very fast. We'd take it to the "Avalanche" sandbar off the Rockaway peninsula and surf waves with the catamaran sailboat in the middle of the ocean.

One day we were sailing with my brother at the tiller. He worked the mainsail while I worked the jib. We had twenty-mile-per-hour winds and were tightening the sails when one of the pontoons started to lift out of the water on our side. We were sitting in the trapeze harnesses attached to the mast, with our feet on the edge of the pontoon, yelling at the top of our lungs, going so fast we were passing motorboats.

Kevin was more adventurous than me by far. I was trying to dump wind so we didn't flip over. He was shouting, "Sheet in—go, go, go!" He loved speed.

He later bought a Trans Am and also owned a one-propeller Cessna with several friends. After taking lessons and earning his pilot's license, he'd fly it from Republic Airport on Long Island to Block Island. It was a five-hour trip by car and ferry, but only a half hour in the plane. I was hesitant to fly with him; by then, I had little kids and didn't want to take unnecessary chances, one of the few areas in our lives where we diverged.

Through it all, our parents accepted the risks we embraced, though I know they worried about us. They never tried to squelch our desire to be firefighters or Kevin's ambition to fly.

When firefighters died in the line of duty, Kevin and I told ourselves privately, *That will never happen to us.* The idea that I'd have to be the one to tell my parents that Kevin had died was inconceivable. But here I was, standing before them, struggling to maintain my composure.

My parents and I huddled in the middle of the living room, dreading the next moment.

"We're not going to find Kevin," I said. "Kevin is gone." Shattered, my parents looked at me with disbelief and held each other's hands.

"Are you sure?" my mom asked softly. My dad said nothing. But I could tell they both were heartbroken. All of us stood there in a sea of emotions not knowing what to do.

I knew my mom would now tell her sister, my aunt Marie, and then my sister, Mary Ellen, in emotional phone calls. Our private sorrow would become part of public grief. There would be no escaping the endless newscasts of the WTC collapse, the attacks, the hunt for the perpetrators. But through the sadness, we found unbelievable kindness. Though my parents never really recovered from the heartbreak, the coming together of family, friends, the Fire Department, and people throughout the world became our strength.

Now I had to go home and tell Ginny and our children that Kevin was gone. When I walked in my front door, Ginny saw the pain on my face and knew that I had broken the news to my parents. Somehow, I got the words out.

Ginny later told me she felt numb, but she could see my pain and sorrow, knowing I had lost my best friend. Our kids got very quiet, in disbelief over losing their favorite uncle. The events were just unimaginable. For several weeks, they believed he might walk in the door at any moment.

11

———

A RACE AGAINST TIME

THE NEXT MORNING, after Dr. Ky plucked more debris from my eyes, I returned to the firehouse.

After learning of our losses, New Yorkers had started showing up at firehouses with donations: cookies, cakes, towels, bottled water. A little boy came to the firehouse with three dollars of his own money to donate. I wasn't sure what we were going to do with so many donations, but it was heartening to see people who wanted to help, to do something from their hearts. The previous night, they had lined the streets in lower Manhattan and clapped as firefighters returned from the Pile to their quarters.

I was going from the apparatus floor to the battalion office when I ran into Captain Tardio on the stairs, who told me that he had seen Kevin in the North Tower.

Engine 7 had made it up to the 30th floor when Tardio had encountered a battalion chief who told everyone to evacuate. They started descending the C stairs. On the 9th floor, they ran into Kevin and members of Engine 33.

My brother and Engine 33 had reached the 32nd floor; after hearing the evacuation order, they'd turned immediately and started down the B stairs. Kevin stopped his team on the 9th floor and told his unit to redirect firefighters from the C stairs to the B stairs, a safer route leading directly out of the building. Captain Tardio encountered Kevin on his way down and made the shift to the B stairs.

"Your brother saved my life. He saved a lot of lives," Tardio said. It was a special moment, and his story of meeting Kevin meant so much to me.

I walked to the Pile picturing that event in my mind. Kevin and the firefighters of Engine 33 had slowed their retreat to direct others to the B stairs, the safest and fastest exit. I wondered how long he had lingered on the 9th floor, knowing that anyone who continued down the C stairwell could get trapped by falling debris or slowed by a more cumbersome way out via the mezzanine. Captain Tardio and many others had made it out. Kevin had given his life to save others.

OUR RESCUE OPERATION ran twenty-four hours a day. Time was of the essence. Studies of earthquake rescues indicated people had survived up to fourteen days in collapses of buildings. We decided to add four days to make sure. After eighteen days of search and rescue, we would move officially into recovery operations.

Firefighters and other rescuers dug and listened for sounds, hoping for a miracle. People went down into the subway tunnels, into the stores in the underground concourses, into many crevices.

Chief Nigro had appointed Frank Cruthers WTC incident commander, with Hayden as his deputy commander. Operations chiefs rotated for each of the four sectors at Ground Zero. I recall it felt like Division 15 Deputy Chief Charlie Blaich and I flipped a coin to determine who would do what role. Blaich became logistics chief and I the planning chief based on who would work best in each function.

The assignment gave me much-needed focus. As planning chief, writing operational plans allocating resources and documenting the recovery process became a major area of my responsibility. To build a command structure my first task was to provide information about the collapse area.

A picture is more easily comprehended than a page full of words. I contacted the FDNY's Geographic Information Systems (GIS) office, called the Phoenix Unit. Captain Justin Werner pulled maps showing city streets and the sixteen-acre site with building footprints of the WTC, then overlaid those with a 75-by-75-foot grid. We divided the area map into four sectors, or divisions, with each four-acre section under the supervision of a deputy chief.

Officers and firefighters were given these paper maps and instructed to mark where they found human remains or equipment on the grid. This system also allowed us to keep track of who was working where, enhancing searchers' safety. All that information had to be logged in at the end of the day by a supervisor.

This time-consuming process slowed us down. But it was vital to know where people and evidence were found, not only for the FDNY in reviewing our tactics, but also for law enforcement for their investigation, engineers determining how the buildings fell, medical examiners trying to identify victims, and families who wanted to know where their loved ones were found.

But the information we were getting was disheartening as, day after day, we found no survivors.

. . .

THE WORLD WAS WATCHING EVENTS at Ground Zero. Though I had no time to view TV, Ginny told me extraordinary pictures were being broadcast of the eerie rubble pile and our desperate efforts to find survivors. People all over the country, all over the world were thinking about us.

President Bush announced he would come to Ground Zero at the end of the week. He had flown over the site but wanted to visit in person for that important national ritual: the presidential walk through the disaster area. The commander in chief wanted to show his support for the victims and signal his determination to hold those responsible accountable.

On the afternoon of Friday, September 14—which had been declared a National Day of Prayer and Remembrance—President Bush arrived at McGuire Air Force Base in New Jersey. Accompanied by New York Governor George Pataki and Mayor Giuliani, he observed the tip of Manhattan by helicopter, along with thirty-seven members of Congress in Marine helicopters. The choppers landed and a long convoy of limos wound its way to the WTC site.

President Bush, accompanied by Pataki, Giuliani, Fire Commissioner Von Essen, and other VIPs, emerged from the vehicles and picked their way across the site. People who had for days been doing backbreaking work, physically lifting chunks of concrete and passing buckets of debris, stopped what they were doing. They looked skeptical, angry, and tired.

Bareheaded, wearing a windbreaker, Bush climbed onto a burned-out fire truck. Someone handed him a bullhorn. He looked around the crowd, at the devastation in all directions. He draped his arm around

Bob Beckwith, a retired firefighter in street clothes and FDNY helmet, who had volunteered to search. I was standing thirty feet away.

"Thank you all," President Bush said. "I want you all to know . . ."

"We can't hear you," someone yelled.

"It can't go any louder," Bush said. He raised his voice. "I want you all to know that America today—America today is on bended knee, in prayer for the people whose lives were lost here, for the workers who work here, for the families who mourn. The nation stands with the good people of New York City and New Jersey and Connecticut, and we mourn the loss of thousands of our citizens."

"We can't hear you!" we shouted.

"I can hear you!" Bush shouted. "I can hear you! The rest of the world hears you. And the people—and the people who knocked these buildings down will hear all of us soon!"

The crowd roared. It was what everyone on the Pile needed to hear.

"The nation sends its love and compassion," he said, "to everybody who is here. Thank you for your hard work." President Bush said, "Thank you for making the nation proud, and may God bless America."

Speaking from the heart, President Bush gave us a sense that we'd get through this.

Then President Bush began walking through the crowd of first responders, which I'm sure drove the Secret Service agents crazy. It made me nervous. The rubble pile was still very dangerous.

The president came over to me. To my right stood Captain Tardio, and on my left, Father Brian Jordan, a childhood friend and Franciscan priest.

The president put both of his hands on my shoulders.

"Mr. President, we can't find my brother," I said, almost choking on the words. "He's a fire lieutenant."

"God will provide," he said, looking at me with deep empathy. He had no political agenda; he really felt my pain.

Bush turned to Captain Tardio, whose grim face looked to him for answers.

"Mr. President, you need to do something about this," Tardio said. Bush leaned over and whispered in his ear, loud enough for me to hear, "We will get them."

He moved on to other people, touching shoulders, shaking hands, looking deeply into faces, obviously very moved. His presidency had been dramatically changed by the attacks of September 11, 2001, and what he saw at Ground Zero. I wondered what was going through his mind. Would we really get the people responsible, and how?

As I grappled with the magnitude and horror of what had happened, I felt overwhelmed. Not just that my brother had been killed, but that so many had died, so much had been destroyed, at the hands of violent extremists. Studying psychology in college and counseling in grad school, I had learned that, for crime victims, losing control is often as devastating as the trauma of the offense. I knew I needed to take back that control, to establish a personal strategy to move forward. I turned my focus to my new job as the Incident Command's planning chief.

Finding survivors was still our main goal. But who was in charge of the recovery effort? According to the City of New York's executive orders, in cases of fires and building collapse, the FDNY is the lead agency in charge.

While the FDNY was officially in charge of the collapse operations, we had to coordinate the efforts of multiple agencies like the NYPD, the Port Authority Police Department (PAPD), the FBI, FEMA, and other city, state, and federal agencies that began arriving in New York to help. It was an enormous challenge.

By early in the second week, we concluded that our Incident Command Post at Ten House on Liberty Street was much too close to the search scene. The operations were getting too big. Our primary mission was searching for survivors, but the command staff along with the chiefs of operations, planning, logistics, and safety needed some distance to focus on the big picture. We were building a system to coordinate our efforts.

Ten House became the Operations Command Post. On September 17, we moved the incident post six blocks to Battalion 1 quarters on Duane Street. What was now called the WTC Incident Command took over one side of our three-story firehouse.

Vehicles were removed from the apparatus floor, which became the meeting room; we built a plywood floor over the concrete that was easier to walk on and put staff offices on the second and third floors. Cushman electric carts ferried us back and forth to the Pile.

I knew we needed a written operations plan with marching orders, so everyone would know what everyone else was doing at Ground Zero, but I was busy handling day-to-day crises. Then twenty-seven people arrived from Arizona: the Southwest Area Incident Management Team (IMT) of the U.S. Forest Service. Called in by FEMA, the team had extensive experience managing responses to wildfires in western states. One morning in the middle of the second week, their planning chief met me in front of the Duane Street firehouse.

"I'm from the Forestry Service," he said. "We have an Incident Management Team."

You're from Forestry? I thought. *The WTC has one surviving tree. How can you help?*

I'm sure my skepticism was obvious. How could managing wildfires translate to an urban disaster?

I must have looked overwhelmed and exhausted. He looked at me with compassion.

"Chief," he said softly, "I know how hard you have been working and it looks like you can use some help. I can help you put together an Incident Action Plan and manage all the other planning functions. We're not going to take over anything."

His empathy and my exhaustion overcame my doubt. I brought him upstairs to meet Chiefs Cruthers and Hayden.

"I'm putting the IMT on the third floor," I said. Nobody blinked an eye. "Okay, Joe," Cruthers said. Hayden nodded. "Whatever you need to do, Joe."

The Southwest IMT was quickly put to work. By September 23, with their help, I wrote our first Incident Action Plan (IAP), which provided interagency coordination for this historic event. Imposing structure through my planning job helped me feel as if I was regaining control.

EVERY MORNING AROUND 7:30 A.M. at the Duane Street firehouse, we held an interagency meeting with as many as a hundred people from numerous agencies with operational tasks at or around Ground Zero. Eventually, we had so many people involved we had to issue identification cards to manage access to the Pile.

During each shift, FDNY had hundreds of firefighters on site, in addition to NYPD and PAPD officers and Urban Search and Rescue teams. The National Guard installed a chain-link fence around the sixteen-acre rubble field and worked with law enforcement on security. The military was still flying over the airspace. The FBI was performing its investigation. The city medical examiner set up a temporary morgue. Four major construction companies worked on dismantling the skeleton of the WTC and debris removal. The EPA and the New York Department of Environmental Protection took air samples.

Before each morning meeting, the Southwest IMT (later relieved by similar teams from Alaska) worked with me to develop an agenda. During those meetings, agency representatives had to answer three questions: What did you accomplish in the last twenty-four hours? What are you doing today? What do you plan to do seventy-two hours out?

Each day, agencies received a new site map that listed operations in each sector and various logistical facilities, and that pointed out dangerous areas.

Unexpected issues arose. For example, the DEP required that every dump truck carting debris to a landfill in Staten Island, where it was sifted through, had to be washed down in order to prevent contaminants from leaving Ground Zero. This wasn't something the FDNY had ever had to handle before on such a large scale, but we figured it out. The New York Sanitation Department was brought in to handle that.

We also had to deal with some unexpected incidents. Below the WTC complex was a huge underground complex of shops, vaults, and concourses. In mid-October, a security team spotted scorch marks on a basement doorway below WTC-4 that hadn't been there a few hours earlier, as if someone had tried to break in. Behind the door was a mountain not of rubble, but nearly a thousand tons of gold and silver, worth an estimated $200 million, being held in a vault in the custodial care of the Bank of Nova Scotia. It was hard to believe that someone was trying to pull off an *Ocean's Eleven*–type heist. A team of thirty firefighters and police officers was mobilized to remove the precious metals.

Those were only a few of the situations that cropped up, and all of the situations created coordination challenges. Almost every time something new occurred, we needed to make sure everyone working on the Pile knew about it, even if they weren't directly involved. We had lost too many people in the attacks, and the last thing we needed was to lose someone else because of a lack of communication. For all our good intentions, a siloed approach had been the norm until I brought in the IMT, but now we were sharing as much information as we could.

While we coordinated efforts at Ground Zero, the Office of Emergency Management oversaw state, federal, international, and private-sector support based out of a building that ran the length of Pier 92 a few miles away. From them, I was able to order daily flyover photographs and LIDAR (light detection and ranging) pictures, three-dimensional images showing the changing elevation of the Pile.

Safety Chief Ron Spadafora visited the Pile every day and held safety meetings each afternoon. Miraculously, we had very few injuries on the site. We provided everyone with a respiratory mask. But at the time, we were getting conflicting information from the EPA that the air was safe. We wouldn't understand the significant environmental health hazards created by the toxic dust and fumes and its effect on first responders until years later.

Some of the most vital people working on the Pile were managers from four major construction companies who brought in ironworkers and cranes to safely dismantle and remove the steel skeletons and large chunks of concrete. At one point, we had twenty-seven cranes at the site.

Since there were no recognizable landmarks on the debris field—which changed daily as material was removed—rescuers relied on the map broken into 75-square-foot grids. Our assumption was that victims would be found together. In reality, some were located in the buildings' footprints, others in the collapse zone, but overall they were found all throughout the complex.

In some cases, we were finding intact bodies. Some firefighters were well preserved because of their bunker gear. But more often, we found body parts, sometimes just equipment, or personal items. Human remains were taken first to the makeshift morgue at the World Financial Center, and later to the regular morgue at Bellevue Hospital.

Our paper method for recording where victims were found proved unwieldy and inexact. If human remains, equipment, or personal items were found, the searchers marked an X on the paper grid showing the location—at best a guess. The task of writing notes by hand then transferring that information to a database only complicated the recovery process.

However, the location of remains found at this enormous crime scene was crucial for medical examiners trying to identify victims and therefore help grieving families. I certainly had a personal interest in finding my brother and members of Engine 33.

On September 26, I held meetings to challenge thirty scientific experts to develop technological alternatives to help streamline the recovery process at the WTC.

After much discussion, we concluded that a handheld GPS device offered the best solution in terms of simplicity and functionality. But there was no device fitting our requirements on the market.

Working with two companies, Symbol Technologies and Links Point, we came up with the solution. The idea was to use a wireless device with a bar code scanner, and programmed with GPS applications, that could be uploaded to a database.

Symbol Technologies had already manufactured something similar that was used by the Red Cross to track blood supplies. Digging around existing inventory, they found a supply of rugged handheld gadgets that could withstand heat, dust, and manhandling by our searchers.

Software engineers with Links Point, based in Norwalk, Connecticut, began working around the clock to create a GPS attachment and software for the device. The two companies accomplished in three days what would normally take three months.

At first, we were worried the GPS component would not work well because of the canyon effect caused by the city's skyscrapers. You need at least three satellites to ensure a good GPS reading. But the large space created by the buildings' collapse opened up the skyline for the devices to connect to the satellites.

Proper use of the device required less than thirty minutes of training—another big plus, especially for people under extreme stress.

Once we were using the new devices, each recovered victim or item was identified by a numbered tag with a bar code. The firefighter scanned the item, then automatically recorded the date, time, and location of the evidence, usually within three meters. The firefighter could choose from a list of categories to describe the item: apparatus (division car, battalion car, engine, ladder, other); human remains (FDNY, law enforcement, civilian); gear/equipment; other. The database meshed the GPS latitude and longitude readings with our grid maps.

We started using our GPS Victim Tracking System on September 28. Two days later, I assigned a team of one officer and six firefighters from the hard-hit Ten House, armed with the devices, to begin patrolling the four quadrants of the site and record findings of victims and equipment. Everyone on the Pile knew to call the Ten House GPS unit to record the location of any recovered person or equipment. Ten House continued this role for the next thirty days; then another unit would assist them.

At the end of each tour, the GPS device was inserted in a synchronization cradle, which automatically uploaded the captured information to a database. Updated several times a day, the database gave us an accurate picture of where remains and equipment were being found. It was tough seeing the multiple red dots on a single map marking bodies, which covered the entire 16-acre rubble field.

This was the first use of this kind of GPS tracking in an urban setting. By the time the search ended months later, firefighters had recorded the location of 4,000 body parts, tagged each with a bar code, then passed that information and the remains to the medical examiner. The FDNY GIS team used this database to show on a map the recovery location of those victims—a tragic and graphic picture of a catastrophic event.

12

UNTHINKABLE LOSSES

A FTER EIGHTEEN DAYS of desperate digging, we'd found no other survivors at the Pile. We had held out hope, but we had to accept reality; thousands of missing people would never go home to their families. As painful as it was to acknowledge this, there was also an element of relief; the urgency that had driven us to find possible survivors had carried its own risk.

Now, as September ended, we moved officially into the next stage: recovery of bodies. We had to remove twelve stories of debris, six above-ground and six underground, which required heavy equipment. With engine noise, working at the Pile was an assault on your ears, nose, and eyes, as the dust and smell of burned concrete lingered.

When a rescuer found human remains, all the equipment was shut down. If the person was a firefighter or uniformed officer, their unit was contacted. The remains were draped with an American flag and members of the company carried out the stretcher as onlookers observed a moment of silence. We treated each person who died with dignity.

The FDNY had needed almost a week to compile a comprehensive list of missing firefighters. The command board in the North Tower had been destroyed. The riding lists on the dashboards of rigs and in officers' pockets had been lost. There had been a change of tours at 9 a.m. the morning of 9/11, which complicated figuring out who had been on the scene. Firefighters who were going off duty got on the rigs trying to do the right thing, but there was no way to track who was where. Firefighters were "riding heavy"—if there was an open seat on a rig, even if they were not on duty, they jumped in a seat and came anyway. Some people responded from home.

We had sent 112 Engines, 58 Ladder trucks, 5 Rescue companies, 7 Squad companies, a Hazmat Unit, a Field Com Unit, 4 Marine Units, dozens of chiefs and civilian leadership, numerous ambulances, and many support units. Overall, about 250 units—roughly half of FDNY's on-duty members—responded that day.

Though Duane Street firehouse had no deaths, other houses in Battalion 1 had suffered terribly. Of those who responded from Ten House, three firefighters and one officer, plus retired Captain James Corrigan, who I had talked to on the morning of 9/11, had died. Engine 6 on Beekman Street lost three firefighters, and the South Street firehouse, Engine 4 and Ladder 15, lost twelve.

FDNY Special Operations Command (SOC), such as Hazmat and Rescue and Squad, had been decimated. In total, seventy-five elite rescue workers were killed. One of them, Firefighter Stephen Siller of SOC Squad 1 in Park Slope, Brooklyn, had just gotten off his shift when he learned about the first plane hitting the North Tower. He grabbed his gear and drove to the Brooklyn-Battery Tunnel, which had been closed to traffic. In full bunker gear, boots, and helmet, he ran through the tunnel to join his unit. He and eleven other members of Squad 1 were killed.

Every night the dispatcher read the list on the radio, I'd recognize a name, or two, or a dozen. It was like a member of your family dying every day. So many were personal friends going back years. Captain Walter Hines and Battalion Chief John Moran had been in my original study group. Walter was a co-owner of a bar in Rockaway where I'd held my bachelor party dinner for the whole firehouse.

The department had suffered a catastrophic loss: 343 members, including our chaplain, two paramedics, and a fire marshal, making it the largest single-day loss of life of any emergency response agency in American history. Among those killed were the highest-ranking, most experienced chiefs, dealing a devastating blow to our ability to reorganize and go forward.

The Port Authority Police Department had lost thirty-seven officers, including Superintendent Ferdinand Morrone and Chief James Romito. The NYPD lost twenty-three police officers, including four sergeants and two detectives.

The ultimate casualty count at the World Trade Center was 2,753, including passengers and crew on the two airplanes. Though we consoled ourselves that our efforts had saved thousands of people who might otherwise have died, the staggering losses were hard to comprehend.

In the days after the attacks, New Yorkers continued leaving flowers, teddy bears, notes, food, and other tokens of sympathy at the doors of firehouses all over the city. Firefighters are seen as heroes, saving rich and poor alike. Residents wanted to show their affection and respect for "their" firehouse, to share in the sorrow.

Large crowds of people gathered on Canal Street, where we had set up a security checkpoint, to encourage rescuers coming from and going to the Pile. They cheered when any first responder vehicle drove through. The Battalion 1 chief's car was replaced, and whenever I passed through their ovations, my heart soared, knowing they appreciated the tough job we were doing.

People from all five boroughs—and from around the region—posted photos of missing civilians and first responders on fences and walls in various spots around Manhattan, hoping against hope that their loved ones were still alive. Some workers at the WTC complex had successfully evacuated, left the island, and found refuge outside the city. But many others had simply disappeared.

At the same time, from across the country and around the world, volunteers started coming together to help families whose loved ones had died or were missing. Pier 94 provided a place for families of the dead and missing to get financial and emotional assistance, while Pier 92 was continuously used for operations. We also took over the Javits Center to house rescue teams.

We wound up splitting the FDNY, at first rotating 1,000 firefighters for two weeks at a time to work on the Pile, and later rotating 600 firefighters and EMS workers every thirty days. At the time, the force had about 11,000 firefighters, plus 4,000 EMS workers and 1,000 civilians. Those not assigned to the Pile responded to emergencies in their neighborhoods. Firefighters worked hundreds of hours of overtime, earning time and a half. The extra income was welcome, but toiling such long hours, especially in a recovery effort involving human loss, was also stressful. Many of our members weren't going home for days at a time.

I worked sixteen hours a day, seven days a week, for two months, only rarely taking a day off. Twenty years of experience helped me manage the anxiety, as did my education. I had a master's degree in theology and the equivalent of half a master's degree in counseling and knew more than many about what to expect in the aftermath. And I was protected to some extent by having a job to accomplish.

But we knew there were risks beyond those on the Pile itself for those working the site. People who had been involved in responding to the Oklahoma City bombing in 1995 warned us that, in the aftermath, survivors were at risk for substance abuse, divorce, depression, and suicide.

I wanted to inoculate myself. Immediately after 9/11, Ginny and I pledged not to drink any wine, beer, or liquor for more than a year—not even a drop of champagne to toast someone at a wedding. To make sure our marriage wasn't impacted, we made a vow to support each other.

Ginny and I could sense the pain our kids, Chrissie and Greg, were experiencing. She tried to keep their schedules as normal as possible. She needed to care for my devastated parents and was working as well. Ginny loved her job, but at times the combined stresses were too much to bear. Though she was glad I had survived, she felt alone in taking care of the kids while I was at the Pile.

She turned to her brother Frankie, her other siblings, and her father for support. Friends from school helped. Her coworkers at the hospital understood what she was going through. Working with cancer patients had taught her patience, endurance, and kindness. She used that knowledge. But it was a dark time for Ginny, the kids, and my parents, as it was for so many grieving families.

In the firehouse, firefighters were experiencing the same pain, as were Jules and Gédéon.

The first time I saw Jules for more than a moment after September 11 was a couple of weeks later, when we sat in my office and he showed me some of the raw footage he had shot. He'd filmed continuously from the moment we answered the odor of gas call all the way through his emotional reunion with Gédéon at the firehouse, missing only eight seconds when he changed tapes. He showed me some of the most breathtaking segments.

We watched together as his camera replayed American Airlines Flight 11, roaring low over the Hudson River, then hitting the North Tower.

Jules had been the only cameraperson in the world to capture that singular, horrific moment. The terror was engraved in my mind forever, even without film to prove it had happened. But seeing the airplane aiming for the tower and disappearing into the building was raw and powerful and extremely disturbing.

From the moment we arrived, Jules had stuck close to my side. Now I was looking through his eyes at myself taking command, giving orders as firefighters entered.

I admired Jules's willingness to keep filming when it would have been safer for him to leave as soon as we arrived at the North Tower. He had not been trained as a firefighter. No one would have thought less of him if he'd left. But Jules stuck it out and recorded an important part of history.

At some point that morning, Jules noticed his hands trembling, whether from exhaustion or mounting fear.

"When I saw firefighters worried, that's when I started to panic," Jules said. "I saw something I'd never, never seen in a firefighter's eyes: uncertainty, disbelief."

I asked Jules if he had footage of me ordering the evacuation of the North Tower. I knew I had done it; I just wanted confirmation. If I was leaving, I had to make sure my firefighters left as well. And there I was, on camera: "Command Post to Tower 1. All units. Evacuate the building." Then I repeated the order. It was good seeing my orders were captured on videotape. This would leave no doubt in anyone's mind that the orders to evacuate were given right away.

Jules showed me the clip of my brother in the lobby. Seeing Kevin silently turn and walk away to do his job, leading Engine 33 up the stairwell, was a very special moment to have on film.

I was grateful to see that my memories of my actions that day meshed with the reality on film. It's easy to second-guess yourself when things are happening quickly.

As I saw in Jules's footage, after the second collapse, we had parted ways. Jules had continued to film for a half hour, walking aimlessly around the treacherous site, asking people if they'd seen a French guy with a camera. People wouldn't look him in the eye, which he took as confirmation that his brother was dead.

"For the next half hour, I'm crying my eyes out, just going up and down the street, asking every firefighter I see, 'Have you seen anyone from Engine 7 and Ladder 1?' In my mind, I've lost my brother, I've lost James [Hanlon]—my best friend—and the entire company's gone."

Jules had no idea that Gédéon was just a block or two away, also wandering around in the dust.

Later that day, as firefighters arrived back at the house, Gédéon captured their joyful reunions before eventually being reunited with Jules. Between them, the brothers had shot astonishing footage against incredible odds.

That footage was important not just for the historical record, but for the FBI as it worked to understand what had happened. About 5 p.m. on 9/11, a man and a woman had appeared at the firehouse and introduced themselves as FBI agents. The New York Field Office of the FBI is just down the block from the firehouse. They had heard Jules had filmed the first plane and asked to see his footage.

Jules and Gédéon agreed to play the film for the agents and immediately took them to their parents' home on the Upper East Side, where they slept when not at the firehouse. Jules's fiancée, Jacqueline, met them at the door, relieved but alarmed by his red eyes and the crust of dust on his hair and clothing.

Jules played the first tape. The group saw his breathtaking film of the hijacked American Airlines plane, silver against a pure blue sky, sweeping low and plowing into the North Tower.

He had not been sure that he had captured the crystal-clear image until the moment he played it for the FBI agents. Jules and Gédéon copied that segment, then gave their other tapes to them. It took a couple of weeks to get the film back from the FBI.

The brothers never hesitated to cooperate with the Bureau. "I'm not a journalist," Jules said. "I wanted to help. My country has been attacked." He'd become an American citizen in 1998 and was honored to assist his country—and to feel he had been chosen to be a witness to history.

Jules and Gédéon returned to the Pile over the next few days to search for survivors, taking turns filming, determined to finish their film. Jules worked with the bucket brigades, balancing on the precarious surface that screeched and groaned and stank. That agonizing sense of helplessness, the smell of death was hard to bear.

Firefighters on the Pile told Jules and Gédéon to film instead of dig. "People need to see this," they said.

It turned out the firefighters needed Jules and Gédéon, too. The guys were struggling with shock and trauma, all grieving, some wrestling with why they had lived when so many of their brothers had died. The list of the dead was growing longer, read on the intradepartmental radio every day. People ate at the kitchen table in silence; no one was sharing stories of that day.

As captain in a firehouse, Ron Schmutzler wore many hats. "Sometimes you're a priest. Sometimes you're a friend. Sometimes you're the disciplinarian." But in the uncharacteristic silence, he was at a loss. He had no idea what to say to the men.

Schmutzler and Tardio knew Jules and Gédéon wanted to talk to the men at some point. So they asked the two filmmakers to begin interviewing the guys in the Duane Street firehouse—or, as people started calling it, the "Miracle House" or "Lucky 7."

Those nicknames wielded a two-edged sword. As New York residents stopped by the firehouse to express their condolences, they were stunned to learn that no one in our team had died, as if their survival diminished what they had done. Nothing could be further from the truth.

Jules and Gédéon agreed, not for the purposes of their film, but to help the firehouse. They were trusted by that point. We'd been through hell together.

At first, the captains thought the men might chat for a few moments in a small upstairs room. But then one of the Naudets came down and told them, "Some of these guys are up here for over an hour and they won't stop talking." The dam holding all their emotions inside had been broken.

Telling stories was what the firehouse did naturally, and now it had a therapeutic role. All of the firefighters were questioning themselves. Had they done the right thing? Could they have saved more people? What emerged were amazing tales of bravery and survival—plus a lot of luck.

I had no hesitation. I trusted Jules. On September 30, I sat with him in that tiny room with green walls that hadn't been painted in four decades. So much had happened in such a short period of time: 102 minutes from the time the first plane hit to the collapse of the North Tower.

As Jules and I walked through the experience again, my emotions were raw. I had been through an extreme event beyond what I could ever have imagined. I had lost my brother and dozens of close friends. The department had been gutted and thousands of people at the World Trade Center were missing. At one point, as I recounted that day, I just had to pause. I remember saying, "I'm not sure if I love the job anymore."

But, for me, storytelling in that little room with Jules helped me start to comprehend the depth of what took place by simply verbalizing what I did and felt. And so it was for the other members of Engine 7, Ladder 1. While the interviews were done individually, it felt like something we were doing together as a firehouse. I was taking control of the memories by sharing my story in my own words.

As bodies were found, the funerals and memorial services began. Among the first, on September 15, had been the funerals for Chief Pete Ganci and Father Mychal Judge, the chief of department and its beloved chaplain.

On September 10, the day before his death, Father Judge had given a homily at the rededication of the Bronx firehouse Engine 73 and Ladder 42. The words of his talk proved he knew the life of firefighters, and they proved prophetic.

"That's the way it is," he told those gathered in the firehouse. "Good days. And bad days. Up days. Down days. Sad days. Happy days. But never a boring day on this job. You do what God has called you to do. You show up. You put one foot in front of another. You get on the rig, and you go out and you do the job—which is a mystery. And a surprise. You have no idea when you get on that rig. No matter how big the call. No matter how small. You have no idea what God is calling you to. But he needs you. He needs me. He needs all of us."

After those first two funeral services, I attended dozens of FDNY memorials and funerals.

As firefighters, we think of ourselves as having two families—our family at home and the firehouse family. Every holiday is divided between time at home with family and working at the firehouse. When a firehouse suffers a line-of-duty death of one of its members, firefighters feel like they have lost a brother or sister and are compelled to take care of the fallen firefighter's grieving family. It is a special part of Fire Department culture to arrange funeral details, provide for the needs of the spouse and children, do necessary repairs to the family's house and vehicles, generally help however we can. It is a deeply emotional time for the firehouse, and everyone bonds together. As the number of line-of-duty deaths rose to 343, the needs became overwhelming. Yet we tried.

In my brother's firehouse, the members of Engine 33 and Ladder 9 cared for ten families of fallen firefighters and fire officers. Since I was working endless hours with no days off, members of Engine 33 drove my father to his prostate cancer treatments. My parents could have taken Access-A-Ride, but just being with a firefighter from my brother's firehouse meant more to them than anything else. It was a way for my parents and the firefighter to feel close to Kevin.

A huge dry-erase board at the firehouse listed each day's wake, funeral, or memorial service for a fallen brother. Some days had a half dozen listed. If you are not working, you are expected to attend your fellow firefighter's funeral. In previous years, it was not unusual for 8,000 firefighters in uniform to line the streets at the funeral to pay our last respects as the caisson—a special fire engine fitted with a lift—carried the firefighter's coffin to the burial place. It was followed by the Emerald Society Pipes and Drums, a band entirely composed of active and retired FDNY firefighters who volunteer their time and pay their own expenses.

Some days, firefighters attended as many as two or three services, grieving for friends lost and experiencing the raw emotions of their deceased fellow firefighters' spouses, parents, siblings, and children. Not only did they attend the funerals, but they also hung bunting, planned the ceremonies, gave eulogies, and helped the family with all arrangements. Anything the parents, widows, or children needed, the firefighters tried to provide.

For months, the FDNY had so many funerals that our members could not go to them all. Firefighters from around the country came to New York for a week at a time to make sure every firefighter had mourners to show their respects.

On November 2, 2001, we held a memorial for my brother at St. Margaret's. We held out hope that we might recover Kevin's body and then we could have a proper funeral. But for now it only seemed right to have some sort of ceremony. The church was packed with family and firefighters in uniform.

The Saturday before 9/11, Jean Nichols, a firefighter from Canada, had come to New York and taken photos of Kevin in uniform. Dressed in full bunker gear and helmet, standing in front of Engine 33, he looked into the camera, handsome, smiling. We used one picture for the memorial card and the altar. There was no procession with a caisson because there was no body. Nobody from Engine 33 had yet been found.

That same day, Mayor Rudy Giuliani went off the deep end. The press, who had lauded him for his strength and resolve in the face of the devastation during his appearances on television, saw another side of him.

On this day, Giuliani pulled rank and announced his decision to close Ground Zero. New York City needed to get back to "normal." Searching the Pile dominated the TV news every night. Businesses in lower Manhattan were shuttered. He wanted to bulldoze the site and move on. He told first responders to abandon recovery efforts and to go home.

The Pile was shrinking, but the removal of tons of debris had slowed as we began going beneath street level. During construction of the WTC complex, a concrete "bathtub" had been built underground to hold back the river. The four construction companies working on salvage operations brought in engineers to shore up the bathtub by driving steel rods into the bedrock to keep water out as they removed structural beams.

The towers extended six stories below grade, and much had been compacted in that zone. The FDNY had lost ninety-one vehicles; many still had yet to be located.

But most importantly, human remains were still being found. An argument erupted with the mayor on one side and the rank-and-file first responders on the other. The mayor had protestors and firefighters demanding that Ground Zero remain open arrested at the site.

I still hoped that my brother's body would be located, and I knew other families felt the same. But Giuliani wouldn't listen to FDNY's pleas to continue recovery operations.

Until families of those lost said something. They told the mayor, "You are not shutting down the site. You will try to recover our loved ones."

Giuliani reversed his decision.

The families also demanded that President Bush and Congress create a commission to understand what had happened on September 11. The National Commission on Terrorist Attacks Upon the United States, also known as the 9/11 Commission, was set up in late 2002.

The controversy was just another stressor in firehouses across the five boroughs. I saw it in the houses in my battalion.

There was anxiety about another "wave of attacks." We considered the possibilities of terrorists exploding dirty bombs, collapsing bridges and tunnels, and attacking shopping malls. What if firefighters battled an arson fire only to be killed by a secondary device planted by a terrorist?

"You could tell there was a lot of fear in the guys' faces," Captain Tardio said. "Nobody ever said, 'I ain't getting on that rig.' You know, the guys still did their job."

But rigs had been destroyed, tools lost, firehouses decimated. Many beloved and respected fire officers and firefighters were dead. Those suddenly promoted had to take on jobs they may not have sought, with the additional burden of training the influx of probies. Would they be safe?

O'Neill frankly admitted he had more trepidation about the job than he had before 9/11. "And it's something I don't like in myself. But it's there. And I don't think you can suffer the kind of losses that we suffered without thinking twice about everything we do as firefighters."

Schmutzler explained to the guys at roll calls and drills how important it was to get back to their purpose. If the bells went off, they were going to a fire.

"If you can't do it, let's get you into counseling, let's put you on light duty," Schmutzler said. "If you have to go sick, you have to go sick. But if you come through that door, and if you put that uniform on, you better be ready to go. You have to come here and be ready to give 110 percent of yourself all the time."

But the captain was also struggling himself. "I didn't know how I was going to get through the days, but I couldn't tell them that. I can honestly say I wasn't there 110 percent."

Captains Tardio and Schmutzler kept their eyes open. But they saw the guys only in the firehouse during their tours. "You don't know what's happening when he goes home," Tardio said.

One night, firefighters from Ladder 1 were at the Pile when they uncovered their own crushed rig. For weeks, recovery efforts had been exhausting and bore little fruit except for persistent coughs and irritated eyes. Schmutzler realized the men needed to find something of value. When they dug out the sign that said "Ladder 1" on the side of the boom on the rig, one of the firefighters put it on his shoulders, and guys followed as he jogged to the firehouse. Everyone cheered as they hung it on the wall.

"I felt like, wow, we still have our truck, you know?" Schmutzler said. "It was just something that we all needed to do." A month later, they would find my battalion car completely destroyed several stories below grade in front of the North Tower. Firefighters removed a badly damaged car door and hung it on the wall of the apparatus floor, along with the sign from Ladder 1 and part of Engine 7.

13

———

FAMILY TIME

AFTER TWO MONTHS OF intense work as chief of planning for the WTC Incident Command, I turned the role over to my colleague Battalion Chief Andy Richter. I needed to get back to my job as a chief in Battalion 1, which was just a few feet away on the other side of the firehouse. I still checked on how the planning section was doing and visited Ground Zero every day that I worked, but I had routine duties.

I also needed a break. In late fall, the state of Hawaii invited the families of NYC firefighters and police officers killed in the WTC attacks to the islands to relax during the first week of December. Hawaiian Airlines donated two airplanes and crews. Hotels provided rooms, and everyone on the islands offered the "Aloha spirit."

Sun, sand, and surf, far away on an idyllic Pacific island—the invitation was tempting, but at first I refused. I felt guilty leaving lower Manhattan. Then I suddenly changed my mind. The Aloha spirit was too welcoming to resist. We needed to get away from the stress, the endless sadness. Ginny, Christine, and Greg were thrilled. As a family, we had never been to Hawaii. It was the longest plane ride we ever took.

As soon as we arrived, we were greeted by a news crew that wanted someone to speak on behalf of the families. I was the highest rank among the FDNY attendees, so I felt a responsibility to step forward. I thanked the Hawaiian people for their generosity—not of their pockets but their hearts, something far more valuable.

Wherever we went, Hawaii took care of us. We went to luaus, snorkeled coral reefs, and learned to surf. We met the governor and the mayor of Honolulu, who showed us the Hawaiian spirit. Tom Brokaw wanted me to do an interview, but we were surfing. I turned him down.

While we were in Honolulu, Christine and Gregory practiced with the local swim club. The Honolulu Fire Department got word of this and took us to the sparsely populated North Shore of Oahu. As we drove up to a dark brown wooden house, we were greeted by eighty-one-year-old Audrey Sutherland. When she was a young, divorced mother of four, Audrey had explored the wild northern coast of Molokai on solo three- and four-mile swims, and later by kayak. Addicted to the experience, she took her kayak all over the world to discover remote coastlines. In 1980 and 1981, she paddled her kayak alone 850 miles from Ketchikan to Skagway in Alaska, journeys that became the basis for *Paddling North*, her third book, a classic in solo seagoing adventure writing.

This slender woman with white hair had lively eyes and a compassionate spirit. Audrey gave us something cool to drink and pointed out Jocko's Beach, where we could go surfing. This beach was a short distance from the famous Banzai Pipeline, a worldwide mecca for serious surfers.

I knew we were in trouble when I learned that the beach was named for her son Jock Sutherland, a surfing legend. The six- to eight-foot waves were beyond my kids' and my new surfing skills. Seeing this, one of her sons took us boogie boarding with fins instead. We swam two hundred yards offshore through the breaking surf, ducking under the white water to catch giant waves, screaming with excitement. Every ride was a solo adventure with nature. Onshore, Ginny watched and thought we were crazy.

During our visit, Audrey—a font of wisdom on self-reliance and optimism—was teaching us something she learned from her adventures, which was to take on challenges with confidence and believe we were going to succeed. In the surf, we tackled big waves, remembering Kevin's adventurous spirit on the Hobie Cat.

When we were leaving, Audrey dubbed us her "New York family" and gave us a copy of her first book, *Paddling My Own Canoe*, published in 1978. It included lessons for this 9/11 family: "The only real antidote for life's pain is inside us. It is the courage within, the ability to build your own fires and find your own peace."

That day, enjoying big waves on the North Shore of Oahu, was the beginning of finding strength in each of us.

I couldn't totally get away from 9/11. In the middle of the week, I was asked to make a short speech on December 7, 2001, in honor of the sixtieth anniversary of the attack on Pearl Harbor. For two days, I racked my brain but couldn't come up with anything to say.

The day before the remembrance, all six hundred family members were shuttled to the USS *Arizona* Memorial for a private tour. The battleship, sunk during the attack, still sits at the bottom of the harbor as a reminder of those who died. As I stood at the memorial, I noticed that oil was still seeping to the surface from the *Arizona*. I watched as 9/11 family members spontaneously took the leis from around their necks and tossed them into the water. At that moment, I knew what I had to say. I started writing my speech on a napkin at lunch.

At the Punchbowl Cemetery for the commemoration, the family members from 9/11, who represented 2,977 victims, were seated behind the podium. In the audience of a few thousand were World War II veterans and family members of those killed on December 7, 1941. The surprise attack had killed 2,403 Americans, including 68 civilians, and injured many more.

I talked about how these two generations mixed together for the first time at the USS *Arizona*, as the oil that seeps from the destroyed battleship gently washed over the delicate and fragrant flowers of the leis tossed in remembrance by the 9/11 families.

"Sixty years ago, families and friends experienced the tragedy of Pearl Harbor and World War II," I said. "We, the families of firefighters, police officers, and rescue workers of 9/11 know what it must have felt like for you, the relatives and surviving friends of the heroes of Pearl Harbor. Those of us from New York City here today are living those same feelings of broken hearts, endless tears, and continual nightmares of America being attacked and losing the ones we love.

"Like sixty years ago, the enemy did not count on America uniting to fight aggression. And today, a new enemy did not count on America and all the people of the world uniting to fight terrorism."

As I'd left the *Arizona* memorial the day before, I had seen a rainbow. "Perhaps it was a rainbow of Pearl Harbor and World Trade Center heroes shining down on us. The heroes we will never forget. It was a rainbow of hope that today's 9/11 generation is just as united as the 1941 generation in the belief that America stands for freedom for all."

The audience was in tears, making it difficult for General Richard

Myers, who had recently been named chairman of the Joint Chiefs of Staff, to follow. But he reminded us of why we should never forget our brave men and women in uniform, both civilian and military.

The week ended with a beautiful luau. We ate traditional Hawaiian food and watched hula dancing. The message was clear: we are all in this together, and by supporting each other, we would get through it. When I looked around, under a cloud of despair that hung over so many families who'd lost their hero first responder, there was a glimmer of hope. I was the lucky one to be with my family, and I took a picture with the Hawaiian dancers who symbolized the Aloha spirit.

The four of us being able to relax in the warm waters of Hawaii became the solution to our sadness. Getting away and having family time together, without other distractions, had been a rare privilege that we needed.

When we got off the plane at JFK Airport in New York, I was hit with the faint but unmistakable smell of Ground Zero. It was a musty odor of damp cement and smoke. Most people would not even notice. But a firefighter's sense of smell is keen. From being down at the Pile, I knew that the odor meant that the underground fires were still burning as the recovery operation continued. We were back to reality.

14

———

BECOMING

W E RETURNED HOME A LITTLE tanned and rested. I was immediately swept back into the routine work of a battalion chief,
watching over my four firehouses. Yet nothing was routine anymore. We
continued to recover bodies at Ground Zero and attend endless funerals
of firefighters as we entered the Christmas season.

Christmas Eve arrived and Santa Claus seemed a little less jolly. At
my sister Mary Ellen's home in Connecticut, we showered my two kids,
Christine and Gregory, and her three children, Meaghan, Caitlin, and
Scott, with gifts. But nothing would make up for the loss of Kevin. My
parents especially seemed like part of their hearts had been torn from
them. I made a slideshow of pictures of my brother so we could remember the good times. There were some smiles among watery eyes.

Seeing the old photos brought home the reality that firefighting had
been part of my life since I was eighteen. The FDNY was my social world;
every day was new and brought a sense of adventure. There was always

something to learn, so it was intellectually stimulating as well. Now everything seemed harder, more uncertain. I needed to find a new path.

As a young boy, I had thought about how others dealt with difficult circumstances with integrity. After the assassinations of Martin Luther King, Jr., and Robert Kennedy in 1968, my teacher assigned *Letter from Birmingham Jail*. I read it in my basement bedroom and was shocked by the idea of segregation. But I was more impressed by Dr. King's willingness to risk everything to stand up to such injustice. Throughout the coverage of his death, news stations would play his "I Have a Dream" speech, which profoundly touched me.

A few months later, I watched Senator Bobby Kennedy's funeral at St. Patrick's Cathedral on TV. His brother Ted quoted Bobby: "Some men see things as they are and ask why. I dream things that never were and ask why not."

Those words etched on my mind the idea not to be limited by my circumstances or by anyone else's expectations. It was the beginning of a budding sense of purpose to speak out for change, even in my small world.

At age twelve, I joined the swim team at the Central Queens YMCA in Jamaica, and later at the Flushing YMCA. We swam year-round and competed throughout the region. We had an eclectic group: guys, girls, Black, brown, white, all swimming with each other. One of the best swimmers on the team was Reynold Trowers, a Black kid who eventually became a doctor. We looked up to fast swimmers and I tried to be like him.

That summer, I invited a bunch of kids from the swim team to Breezy Point for the day. The beach had private security; only visitors invited by guests could enter. Worried that my Black and Latino guests might get hassled, I went to the guardhouse and made sure they knew my group of friends had been invited.

As I began thinking about a career, being a professional firefighter didn't occur to me, though Queens was a popular neighborhood for members of the FDNY and NYPD. I knew I wanted to find a path that would allow me to serve others.

Since my illness at age seven, I had idolized Dr. John Scalzo. He and his colleagues had saved my life. For years, I'd wanted to be a doctor, but Dr. Scalzo passed away a couple of years after my illness. If he hadn't, I probably would have thought more about medical school.

So I turned to my other role models: priests who were family friends. They were well educated, interesting, and funny. In the late sixties, being a priest seemed like a radical way to make a difference, especially after Vatican II. The focus was on engaging in dialogue with other religions; changing the mass from Latin to English had a big impact on me, making it more personal.

In ninth grade, I attended Cathedral Prep in Elmhurst; with only two hundred students, the highly rated high school was considered a minor seminary. Since my parents couldn't afford the tuition, our local parish priest, Father Anthony Mueller, paid for part of my education out of his own pocket. I made As and B+s but was never the academic star—more of an idealistic misfit. I ran track and then devoted my athletic time to competitive swimming at the Flushing YMCA. As part of the required community service, I worked with special-needs kids. I always looked for that different path. But I didn't read the fine print—the part about priests not getting married.

After graduating from high school in 1974, I enrolled in Cathedral College of the Immaculate Conception in Douglaston, Queens, to pursue a degree in psychology with a minor in philosophy. The priesthood was my future goal.

I lived on campus, about ten miles from my parents' house, and set school records on the swim team. My teammates and I would rent a Winnebago and drive to Florida on spring break. We would attend Easter vigil at Cathedral, then set off on a wild adventure down south, which gave new meaning to going on "retreat."

During the summers, I continued working as a lifeguard at Riis Park, where each area of the beach had its own flavor, a sampling of New York City within a one-mile stretch of sand. The first beach permitted nudity. There were beaches where people gathered as families; beaches where LGBTQ folks openly mingled. African Americans celebrated their roots and music; Latinos did the same. There was also a beach for special-needs swimmers. I worked one of the busiest, Bay 9, which was predominantly Latino, so I got to use my high school Spanish. And every culture brought its own cuisine to the beach. The Puerto Rican and South American families introduced me to wonderful food.

Like my parents—and like most people in the area of Queens where I grew up—people on the beaches were working class. Despite the crowding, and the multitude of ethnicities, people got along well. Something about being in the water made all the difference.

The ocean currents could be treacherous, and I made many rescues. With experience, I could predict where and when people would get in trouble. Better to blow my whistle and prevent a problem than have to make a swimming rescue with a torpedo buoy strapped across my shoulder.

I got certified as a water safety instructor with a specialty in teaching water safety to special-needs kids. One warm summer day, a teenage boy who couldn't walk because of an accident came to the beach and desperately wanted to go into the water. I dragged his wheelchair into the surf to where I could lift him up, then got him out past the breakers. I told him to stand up in the chest-deep water.

He looked at me with anger and sadness—like, *How could you be so mean?* since I knew he was paralyzed.

"Trust me," I said. "You can do this." I pulled him up, and in the buoyant seawater he could stand. He loved it. We stayed in the water for at least three hours. That became a lifelong metaphor for me: *Water is the solution.*

I CONTINUED TRAINING with the Vollies. The mid-1970s were the FDNY's war years, as waves of arson swept the city, especially in the South Bronx, Brooklyn, and Harlem. As people moved to the suburbs, owners who couldn't make money on their apartments decided to torch them for the insurance money. It was shocking to me, as a member of a volunteer fire department, to learn that landlords and developers were burning poor neighborhoods for profit. News stories of firefighters running into flames to rescue those in danger were a reminder of how brave, well-trained fire-fighters could make a difference.

When I was a junior in college, someone brought a bunch of applications for the FDNY to our Tuesday night drill at the Vollies. Tens of thousands of people took the FDNY test each time it was offered, competing for only a couple of thousand jobs. Scheduled for the summer of 1977, the test was like the Olympics: you got a shot at it only once every four years.

The competition was fierce because it was a popular civil service job. New Yorkers looked on the FDNY as the best fire department in the world, and on its firefighters as the bravest.

With roots in volunteer fire squads scattered around the region during Colonial times, the FDNY had been founded as an official force with paid, well-trained firefighters in 1865. For hundreds of years, those brave firefighters played an important part in the city's history. They battled the Great Fire of 1776 during the Revolutionary War, as well as the Great Fire of 1835, which destroyed Wall Street. After the FDNY was founded, its firefighters fought the Brooklyn Theatre fire of 1876 that killed nearly 300 people and the *General Slocum* ship fire of 1904, in which 1,021 passengers and crew died. The Triangle Shirtwaist Factory fire of 1911, which took the lives of 146 garment workers, triggered the adoption of New York City's fire prevention codes. In 1990, an irate person threw a gallon of gasoline up the stairs, killing 87 people at the Happy Land social club fire in the Bronx.

In 1977, when I decided to train hard for both the physical and written parts of the test, I had no idea that I would be challenged to the limits of my abilities. I joked that I was taking the FDNY test as an insurance policy in case I liked those girls on the beach too much. (By now, I had read the fine print about priests and celibacy.)

Between swimming, lifeguarding, and the Vollies, I was in good physical shape. But the FDNY required a much higher level of strength and endurance. The test required applicants to carry a 125-pound dummy up a flight of stairs and back down; hang from a high bar for a minimum of a minute; walk on a four-inch ledge with a twenty-pound pack on your back; and run an obstacle course, then pull yourself over a flat eight-foot wall, not to mention a mile run. The test was more about sifting through applicants than firefighting. I used the college facility to train with some friends for weeks.

The FDNY did the physical part of the test at the Brooklyn Armory. I was pretty confident I had done well, but when I got my results, there were 2,000 applicants who had scored higher than I did. That meant it would be two years before I'd even get called for an interview. That's how tight the scoring was. I put a future with the FDNY out of my mind.

When I graduated from college in 1978, the commencement speaker was Mario Cuomo, who had just lost the New York City mayoral election to Ed Koch; Cuomo would later be elected governor of New York for three terms. A dynamic, inspirational speaker, he talked about a life of service by starting with the individual. That appealed to my desire to pursue a higher purpose.

For graduate school, I enrolled in the Seminary of the Immaculate Conception in Huntington, Long Island, fifty miles from my parents' house. A little more expansion of my small world. I planned to get a master's degree in divinity, with an additional concentration in counseling.

Every semester, we had to do community work. Most of my peers taught religious education in a parish. In some rich parishes, the men studying for the priesthood were doted on, encouraged with gifts. I had become a bit more radical, pushing the idea of helping the poor, reaching out to those who were hurting. I did my community service in the Suffolk County jails, walking the tiers of the cells, talking to people awaiting trial for all kinds of crimes. The guards opened the door and locked me inside, but I never felt at risk. The people behind bars were willing to tell me their stories and I would listen. I would reach through the bars of their cells to shake their hands.

On the less serious side, in my second year, I became the bartender/manager for the campus pub, keeping it open late. It is amazing how you can solve the problems of the world late at night over a beer.

After two years at seminary, we each had to do a year-long internship in a parish. We were supposed to help out at mass, teach religious education, do home visitations. I picked St. Augustine's, a poor trilingual parish in Brooklyn—English, Spanish, and Haitian Creole. We would give out food to many who were so grateful. I also worked at a Lutheran medical center as a student chaplain in that hospital's clinical pastoral education program, which was worth graduate credits in counseling. I visited with patients as they struggled with illness or injuries. Wearing an intern's white lab coat, I listened to the concerns of patients, visitors, and staff, whatever their religious beliefs.

Throughout the seminary, I was always the guy who thought differently. I wrestled with God and couldn't understand why God allowed me to have uncertainty if he was calling me to be a priest. In that wrestling, really getting in the mud, I kept asking, *God, do you want me to be a priest or get married? What are you calling me to do with my life?*

And then I got an answer—sort of.

In the summer of 1981, I finished my intern work in a parish for the year and got the call from the FDNY.

I requested a leave of absence for two years, arguing that being a firefighter would help in my formation. But what the Fire Department wanted to do was shape me in a different image. They were looking to create ordinary heroes.

THE SIX-WEEK FIRE ACADEMY ON Randall's Island, from early September to the first week of October, resembled military boot camp, with short haircuts and instructors screaming in your face. Coming from an academic background, I had to adjust.

Training to be a firefighter was like training to be a soldier in the Army: learning to follow orders, to use your tools properly, and to understand the wiles of your very dangerous enemy—fire.

But it was also fun, always a challenge, and never boring.

We ran, did calisthenics, and read manuals on the physics and behavior of fires. How does the fire grow? What's happening to a room on fire? How is the building being destroyed while you are going in? The sheer amount of material was overwhelming, like drinking from a firehose. The science of fire and the skills of firefighting have grown exponentially. New firefighters now spend four or five months in the academy.

Understanding fire behavior and firefighting procedures gave us a base knowledge of what to expect. This allowed us to recognize the anomalies and adjust to them. Overcoming fear by familiarization was the key to developing a firefighter. Fear was now a tool to combat the unexpected.

The academy taught us to pull hose, climb ladders, search smoke-filled rooms, and use the SCBAs. There was a term, "smoke-eaters," for older firefighters who knew how long they could last without an air mask before they passed out. That sounded like a bad idea. Carbon monoxide is deadly. I'd rather wear my SCBA and make it last longer by controlling my breathing, an old scuba diving trick.

We learned to properly hold a Halligan tool (named for a chief who joined the FDNY in 1916) while someone else hit it with an ax to force a door open. And we climbed hundred-foot aerial ladders carrying hose. I had to overcome any latent fear of heights. Instructors would put a ten-foot scaling ladder flat up against the building. We had to climb straight up to enter a window, reposition the ladder into the next window, and climb that.

We also had to rappel down from the roof of a six-story building, a tactic sometimes used to rescue people who were trapped. It was terrifying looking over the edge, even with a net below. Eventually, it became fun. I never did it at a fire scene myself, but I commanded at a job where firefighters rappelled down a building to save a person who otherwise would have died.

Always our instructors stressed safety. When I started, the turnout coat was very light and not protective. Water would go down into your boots. You'd get the top of your ears burned, a sign you needed to get out. We changed to bunker pants and a coat made of Nomex with a heavy thermal lining, and these days a Nomex hood for head and ear protection. Other equipment, such as thermal cameras, which show the location of the fire, have improved safety.

There were other lessons. During training for first aid, I corrected the instructor who was talking about hyperthermia. I had literally memorized the manual while competing in first aid with the Vollies. He went off on me, but later apologized and said I was right. Even so, I learned being right isn't everything. In the fire academy, the firehouse, and life, creating a team was paramount.

My parents came to my graduation from the academy. My father was so proud and my mother was supportive, but I'm sure Mom thought I was crazy. My brother was intrigued. After graduating from Marist College in Poughkeepsie, New York, Kevin had become a paramedic and rode with ambulances for the NYC Health and Hospitals Corporation. He was so skilled that doctors would ask him to intubate patients in the emergency department. We had many discussions about how to get the Fire Department to take over the relatively young Emergency Medical Services (EMS). FDNY did so in 1996.

As a probie, I was assigned to Engine 234, which was in the same firehouse with Ladder 123 and Battalion 38, in Crown Heights, in the middle of Brooklyn on the corner of St. John's Place and Schenectady Avenue. This was a poor, congested neighborhood made up of African

Americans and Hasidic Jews. St. John's Place East was one of the busiest firehouses in the city for occupied structural fires.

Every FDNY firehouse grabs its personality from the community, especially in distinctly ethnic areas like Crown Heights, Harlem, Chinatown, and Little Italy. Hundreds of languages are spoken in New York, and each firehouse and EMS station has its own culture, depending on the population and the work it does. High-rises or tenements? Industrial or residential? Apartment buildings or private dwellings? Many firehouses interact a lot with school kids, teaching them "stop, drop, and roll" and showing them the fire trucks. But wherever you are, there is always an emotional connection to the community, symbolized by the silhouette of the firefighter in a helmet searching for people who need help—a symbol of hope.

My first firehouse had a lot of minority firefighters. The Vulcan Society, the fraternal order for African American firefighters within the department, had its building around the corner. I didn't realize until later when I got promoted and worked in different firehouses that the FDNY was 90 percent white at that time. In January 1982, the first women were accepted by the department as the result of sex discrimination lawsuits. My initial firehouse received one of the early female firefighters, who was exceptional. Today, diversity is our goal, to better serve our city's wonderful mix of cultures and people.

For a year, I wore a helmet with an orange front patch that read, "Prob Firefighter," to distinguish me from full-fledged firefighters. Probies are inexperienced and, at times, dangerous to themselves. Firefighting requires a set of skills, but it is also an art that can only be developed over time with experience.

At a fire scene, I often watched the most senior person in the company to see what he would do. I remember one older firefighter standing in front of a building as it burned, arms crossed, taking it all in. He took a moment to think, then went to the location where he expected to find a victim. He made the rescue and got a medal for it.

Firefighting is, above all else, learning to control your physical and emotional reactions as you focus on the task at hand. When an alarm comes into the firehouse, you hear a tone alert. Your heart starts to pound. You throw on your gear and jump on the rig. You hear loud sirens in the background as you listen to the radio, trying to glean bits of information. Is someone trapped? As adrenaline flows, your mind races, thinking even before you get to the scene: *What do I need to do to get that person out?*

Some runs were extremely dangerous—fire blowing out a window, down a hallway, multiple people trapped, no easy access. In every big fire, it was important to have a sense of fear, which is a warning device. Fear allows you to pick up on information that helps you follow through on your mission. You develop a sense of fear (awareness) and a sense of courage (calmness) at the same time. They are not two separate elements. They come together in that moment of danger.

I worried about people who didn't have that fear. The smartest firefighters are constantly aware of the hazard as they move into situations where everybody else is running away.

One of my first fires in an occupied residential structure was an accidental blaze in a tenement building dating back to the early 1900s. We didn't know the origin of the fire. We were on the second or third floor. The Ladder searched the apartment and told us in the Engine that the fire was in a back room. I was on the nozzle.

As a nozzle firefighter, going up against fire can be like fighting a wild animal that has a mind of its own. Flames race across the ceiling as heat surrounds you. Disintegrating plaster falls as the beast tries to outdo your maneuvers. Its intention is to consume everything in its path, leaving charred remains.

When we entered, the smoke was so black I couldn't see. Somehow, I held on to the nozzle, and squatting down, duckwalked into the room to stay below the heat. Other firefighters were pushing me from behind, keeping the hose straight. Then, while on my knees, gripping the hose with all my power, I hit the ceiling with the water, rotating the nozzle clockwise. I felt the intense heat and saw a glow in the corner. I quickly shot it with a blast of water, driving the flames back.

Outside, the Ladder was breaking windows to enter and search, and opening the roof bulkhead door to let out the smoke. The room started to clear. Now able to see, we continued to extinguish little pockets of fire. Not only did I put out my first fire, I learned that teamwork was absolutely necessary.

In my first few years, I was going to a lot of fires and loved the excitement, the adrenaline rush, and the FDNY culture. A "10-75"—a working fire—would bring four Engines and two Ladders, two chiefs, a Rescue, and a Squad to the scene. The FDNY has a lot of resources, so it sends lots of people. You can always turn them around—but if you need them, you can't wait.

The St. John's East firehouse was in a crime-ridden neighborhood with shootings about once a week, sometimes more. Several times, we scurried into the street in front of the firehouse to treat someone with a gunshot wound. We threw the victim in the back of the chief's SUV and raced to the hospital in our makeshift ambulance while I did CPR.

The housewatch for Engine 234 was a six-foot-square fishbowl with large plate-glass windows in one corner of the building. Though people generally like firefighters, we were afraid we'd catch a stray round, so we installed bulletproof glass behind our housewatch windows. Police officers sometimes dashed into the firehouse to get off the street. They'd hang up their gun belts and we'd feed them.

It wasn't always about firefighting.

In February 1983, a blizzard dumped two feet of snow on New York City. The only thing moving on most roads were fire trucks. We got called to a house where a seventeen-year-old pregnant woman had gone into labor.

By then, I had been certified as an EMT; we had another EMT and an obstetrics kit on the rig. The baby was coming so fast, and the ambulance couldn't make it through the snow. We had to deliver the baby ourselves.

I kept talking to the mother as I was delivering her baby, reassuring her that she could do this. The head emerged, followed quickly by the baby's body. I cradled the tiny girl, suctioned her mouth, and heard her cry. It was the most beautiful sound I'd ever heard. I cut the umbilical cord, wrapped the baby in blankets, and gave her to the mom. We then bundled up mother and child and carried them up the block to an ambulance waiting on the main road. Plowing through heavy snow, we followed the ambulance to make sure they got to the hospital.

The next day, the newspapers wanted to do a story on the blizzard baby. When I walked into the hospital room, the mother didn't acknowledge me at all. I was crushed. But when I started talking, she immediately recognized my voice and started smiling. A hospital nurse brought the newborn out, and we posed for photos. We'd made a difference for this young family. They would face enough challenges ahead of them, but they were at least healthy, which made me and my fellow firefighters feel very special and part of their lives.

After every fire and emergency run, we returned to the firehouse and

I am all smiles for a family picture with my sister, Mary Ellen, and brother, Kevin, when we were kids in the 1960s. We were very close, jumping into our parents' bed early in the morning and playing at the beach together.

In 1999, Kevin was promoted to lieutenant, making my parents and me so proud of him. The two of us shared a love for the job, responding to fires, medical calls, and emergencies. We both now would work in lower Manhattan.

My wedding day with Ginny was one of the happiest days of my life. Our love for each other would grow in ways we could not imagine as we faced life's challenges and shared so many good times.

With Ginny being a nurse and me a firefighter, our schedules sometimes meant one person got home when the other headed off to work. But as crazy as it was, one of us was always at home with the kids.

Fast-forward thirty years, our daughter, Christine, is a registered nurse caring for bone-marrow transplant patients, and our son, Greg, is a director of cybersecurity.

By luck, on September 8, my brother Kevin's picture was taken at his firehouse in front of Engine 33. Just three days later, Kevin and his firefighters responded to the North Tower on my first transmission that a plane crashed into the World Trade Center.

08:46 A.M.

I was standing in the street for an odor of gas emergency. Suddenly I heard jet engines. Then I watched the first plane aim and crash into the World Trade Center. Immediately I knew this was a terrorist attack and thousands of people were in their greatest moment of need. I transmitted multiple alarms. As the first chief to arrive, I took command to manage the escalating crisis in the North Tower.

Filmmaker Jules Naudet captured the only pictures of the first plane crashing into the WTC and our operations inside the lobby of the North Tower.

With a 110-story skyscraper fire, I communicated our operational plans to the firefighters, EMS personnel, and others streaming into the lobby.

09:03 A.M.

Our problems have just doubled when a second plane crashed into the South Tower. Now we had two 110-story buildings on fire with thousands of people trapped.

We chiefs urgently discussed how to split our forces to manage both WTC Towers. Chief Peter Hayden and I would stay in the North Tower, while Chiefs Donald Burns and Orio Palmer would go to the South Tower.

In the lobby of the North Tower, Assistant Chief Joe Callan, Deputy Chief Hayden, and I commanded one of the world's most complex events. As firefighters and fire officers came in, they knew they were going to the largest and most dangerous fire of their lives. They came up to me and asked, "How can I help?"

One of those fire officers who reported to me was my brother, Kevin. We looked at each other, wondering if we would be okay. Then I told him to go up. He quietly turned and led his firefighters upstairs to evacuate occupants and rescue those trapped.

Kevin, the fire lieutenant, on the left, is with his Engine 33 firefighters, who are to his right.

Father Mychal Judge, FDNY's beloved chaplain, was praying for all of us in the lobby of the North Tower. Moments later, I would find his body in the darkness of the first collapse.

9:59 A.M.

I heard a loud rumbling sound. In complete darkness, I made a critical decision to pull firefighters out of the North Tower:

"Command to all units in Tower One, evacuate the building."

What I did not know at that moment was that the South Tower collapsed and time was running out.

The North Tower collapsed twenty-nine minutes after the South Tower. At the WTC, 2,753 were killed, including 343 FDNY firefighters. In total, the 9/11 attacks killed 2,977 people. Fires burned for four months beneath the building skeletons of Ground Zero. We continued recovery efforts until we reached the bottom of the Pile on May 30, 2002.

Photo by ©GaryMarlonSuson

One of the most difficult things I did at Ground Zero was on Super Bowl Sunday, 2002, when I recovered my brother Kevin's body, in his bunker gear, near the B stairs of the North Tower. All work on the Pile stopped, and first responders saluted as Engine 33 and I carried my brother to his final journey home.

Three days after the attacks, President Bush and I had an emotional moment when he spoke with me at Ground Zero. On my right was Captain Dennis Tardio, from Engine 7, and on my left was Father Brian Jordan. A year later, the president and I had a hamburger in the White House's kitchen.

Six month after 9/11, the Smithsonian asked if I would donate my fire gear and my brother's officer tool. Secretary Hillary Clinton, then my New York senator, was with me at the opening of the 9/11 exhibition. My helmet is now in the 9/11 Memorial Museum.

I was proud to walk alongside my aide Ray Pfeifer, who was struggling with 9/11 cancer, as we joined thousands of FDNY firefighters marching up Fifth Avenue at New York's St. Patrick's Day Parade.

FDNY partnering with the U.S. Military Academy at West Point to develop future leaders. Left to right: Chiefs Michael Weinlein, Peter Hayden, and Frank Cruthers; Major Reid Sawyer; Fire Commissioner Nicholas Scoppetta; Chiefs John Norman and Sal Cassano; Deputy Commissioner Don Shacknai; Senior Advisor Kate Frucher; and me.

DUANE STREET FIREHOUSE

We never know the day when history will choose us. 9/11 was that day. It was a miracle that all of us from Engine 7, Ladder 1, and Battalion 1 and the Naudet brothers survived the collapse of the WTC, which allowed us to tell our story.

Despite everything that we have been through, from terrorist attacks to hurricanes, Ginny and I love being with each other. Here we are relaxing by sailing across Jamaica Bay and into the Atlantic Ocean off the Rockaways.

talked. What went right, what went wrong, and how to fix it. That was how the firehouse built teamwork and resiliency. Somebody might write a memo, do a magazine article, or suggest a drill. Everyone, no matter their rank, participated.

Unfortunately, line-of-duty death was not uncommon. In 1978, three years before I joined, six FDNY firefighters, including a battalion chief, were killed in a five-alarm blaze at the Waldbaum's supermarket in Brooklyn when the roof collapsed. Many more were injured.

When even one firefighter is killed in the line of duty, it is traumatic for the whole department.

Once a year, in the first week of June, the FDNY celebrates Medal Day on the steps of City Hall. It is a day on which we recognize acts of bravery and initiative. Firehouse members and families come out to cheer their fellow medal recipients. For each medal, a short description of the heroic act is read. We marvel at their courage and wonder how they could even be alive after running into such dangerous circumstances.

For the firefighters receiving the medal, the rescue is exciting but at the same time part of the job. When they are recognized by their peers, who understand exactly what dangers and challenges they face, they feel appreciated and understood by those who truly get it. Running into danger requires courage and training. When it's done, firefighters feel privileged to have an opportunity to make a difference in someone's life, and that is extraordinary.

I WORKED AS A FIREFIGHTER for six years at St. John's East, three years in Engine 234 and the other three in Ladder 123. Occasionally, I was sent to other firehouses in the battalion to balance manpower. Over time,

I changed, not only in my level of skill, but also in my physical reactions to danger, my intuition. I learned to listen to the fear, but control it to do what I had to do.

As a firefighter often working in darkness, your other senses become keener as you listen for moaning victims or sense a temperature change. Experienced firefighters are like bloodhounds. Even from a mile away, we can tell if it's a real fire or a false alarm. A burning car and a burning building don't smell the same.

Working on the Fourth of July in the 1980s meant running all night chasing blazes set by fireworks, which would fly into a window and burn very quickly. After putting it out, we could go to the roof and be able to pick out the next fire.

Every now and then, I'd be detailed to be the chief's aide in Battalion 38. The chief is like a conductor of an orchestra, getting everyone to work together. One time, as we were driving between firehouses, we received a run a block away and got to a fire before the units. I told the chief I'd go inside and find out what was happening. The idea is to find any people as soon as possible. Fire rapidly spreads, so every minute counts.

I did a quick search of the fire apartment and found an elderly woman trapped in a bedroom, frozen in terror.

Over the years, I'd learned that if you gave people clear direction, they would follow it.

I told her what we were going to do, guided her past the flames while shielding her with my coat, and got her out before we had water on the fire. Though it wasn't a terribly dangerous rescue, I received a citation and a ribbon on my jacket.

I made lieutenant in August 1987 with a little less than six years on the job. On my first day as a lieutenant, an older firefighter looked at me and said, "You look younger than my son. I need to retire." And he did.

As an officer, it's not enough to know what to do. You become responsible for firefighters and their safety.

When a fire becomes more and more complex, and we have to make decisions, the stress level increases. One of the most difficult times as an officer is receiving a "mayday" message, a signal that the firefighter is in trouble. "Mayday, mayday, mayday"—repeated three times—means the firefighter is trapped, doesn't know their way out of the building, or is seriously injured. It tells the other firefighters to stop talking on the radio and listen. In just three words, a lot is being communicated. Something is seriously wrong—a life-or-death situation.

In a type of checklist, officers need to know the firefighter's location, their unit, the assignment, and what resources are available so we can make sure the firefighter gets out of the building alive. Leadership is more than giving orders. It's about sharing the danger and making critical decisions.

I bounced around firehouses for a year covering open spots, then got a permanent slot in Ladder 128, which was quartered with Engine 259 and Battalion 45, located directly across the street from Calvary Cemetery in Sunnyside Queens—thus the nickname "Tombstone Territory."

Ladder 128 was slower than my Brooklyn firehouse, near two expressways, and one of the few Ladder companies at the time to have a Hurst tool, the so-called "Jaws of Life" apparatus. We worked a lot of car accidents and had to use it to pry metal apart to free the injured. You could read the manual all you wanted, but only practice gave you proficiency with the tool. A nearby junkyard processed vehicles. I'd order ten cars and we'd cut them up for practice. Everybody loved a hands-on drill. Occasionally we got into power struggles with police responders, who also had Hurst tools. Who gets to do the rescue?

I was starting to recognize patterns. Under stress, groups turn to their own because that's who they are more comfortable with. I'd seen that dynamic play out on the street at major fire scenes and emergencies, even car accidents. To overcome it, I dealt with the local police precincts, talking to lieutenants and captains to break down these barriers.

After my promotion to captain, I often covered Engine 40, Ladder 35, in the Lincoln Square area. There, I met Ray Pfeifer, a young firefighter. Though our last names were the same, we weren't related. A tall muscular guy with tousled blond hair, Ray was the unofficial mayor of the firehouse, with a big personality and so well connected that he knew how to get anything done. The two Pfeifers became good friends.

A lot of firefighters don't want to work in Manhattan. They can't afford housing, and heavy traffic adds hours to their commutes. But I loved it. Instead of inspecting warehouses, we'd check out a loft, Lincoln Center, or a luxury high-rise office building. We'd do night inspections of theaters while a production was going on, standing backstage at plays no one could get a ticket to, making sure the doors were open and safety procedures were being followed while watching the actors onstage.

I put in as permanent captain for Engine 40, Ray's house, but another captain got it. I was assigned to Engine 307, a busy firehouse in Jackson Heights, Queens, a mixed neighborhood with a majority Latino population. The company next to us was Ladder 138, where I met Orio Palmer, also a captain.

The area was overpopulated. Two families would crowd into an apartment designed for one. We'd see illegal apartments in the basement, storage of combustibles in unsafe surroundings, and other circumstances that created dangerous fires.

Throughout a firefighter's career, going down a hallway or into a staircase is one of the most dangerous things you can do. When you are leading a team, there needs to be a high level of trust. Firefighters must believe you are not going to ask them to do anything that you wouldn't do.

In one building, I was taking firefighters down an interior stairway into a basement fire when something didn't feel right. Sensing sudden extreme heat, I pulled everyone out. Fire roared up the stairs. I learned another unit had opened a cellar door in the back, feeding air to the flames. We managed to retreat with no injuries, but I was furious at the person who did that and didn't tell me. They could have killed my unit.

Over the years, I learned to combine knowledge with experience. I worked in busy firehouses and went to many fires, which is the best teacher. But no two fires are alike, so experience is not enough. For me, this meant spending twenty-five hours a week studying fire procedures and laws for promotion tests as well as to be a better fire officer.

Kevin had decided to take the FDNY test in 1989. Though Kevin loved being a paramedic, he wanted the adventure and excitement of firefighting. I helped train him and some of his friends. As with me, it took two years for the FDNY to call him up. I attended his swearing-in ceremony and graduation from the fire academy and felt enormous pride in my kid brother. Assigned to Ladder 108, a fairly busy house in Williamsburg, Brooklyn, Kevin continued moonlighting as a paramedic.

I made battalion chief in 1997 and bounced around Manhattan firehouses a bit before I got assigned to Battalion 1, with quarters in the Duane Street firehouse. As a captain, you hear everyone's problems; only the serious stuff comes to you as a chief. I was still in the firehouse yet in a middle-management position, the best of all worlds. But the responsibility for the safety of dozens of firefighters at a fire is not something to take lightly.

I loved being a battalion chief. My brother and I were having the time of our lives in FDNY. Promoted to lieutenant in 1999, Kevin had been assigned to Engine 33 on Great Jones Street in NoHo (North of Houston), sometimes referred to as the Bowery U, since NYU was just down the block. It is a historic firehouse not far from Duane Street. We'd run into each other on multiple alarms.

Joining the FDNY had worked out perfectly for Kevin. NoHo was an exciting neighborhood for a single guy. His firehouse had a good reputation. He had bought my aunt Nell's house, two houses from where we grew up. Though he had not yet married, he had girlfriends.

We would help each other with house renovations. But we made a pact not to do any renovations in the summer. Instead, we went sailing. He also introduced my kids to sailing. My rule was, if you could swim across the bay—about a mile—you could go out on the boat with Uncle Kevin. My kids said, "No problem. How fast?"

In the late summer of 2001, Kevin cut back on socializing so he could study for the captain's test. He took vacation time and traded mutual tours to get blocks of days off. That's why it was surprising when I saw him in the lobby of the North Tower. I'd thought he was off duty.

15

———

SAYING GOODBYE

AFTER BEING STRETCHED TO MY limits in 2001, I simply wanted to get back to something that resembled a normal way of life in the new year. My kids returned to their routines of school and swimming practices. At work, I was now just a battalion chief in Battalion 1. Though I would take a ride to Ground Zero during each tour to check on progress, my life appeared to be as it had been.

On Sunday, February 3, 2002, the guys in the firehouse kitchen on Duane Street were preparing the evening meal as they watched the Super Bowl. I was doing a night tour when I received a phone call from the FDNY dispatcher to report to the Pile immediately. The dispatcher wouldn't give me any other information, which was a little strange.

As my aide drove me to Ground Zero, I did not say a word. In my heart, I knew they had found the remains of my brother. That was something every family desperately wanted and, at the same time, dreaded.

I had made peace with myself walking along West Street, understanding that my brother had been killed. But I knew finding his body would rip off the scab that had formed over that wound.

The winter night was cold and dark, but the WTC floodlights blazed on the landscape of rubble. When I arrived at the site, I was approached by Lee Ielpi, a retired firefighter from Rescue 2, searching for his son, who'd responded as a firefighter on 9/11. Somberly, he told me they had found Kevin. I said nothing.

The sixteen-acre site, now several stories below grade, looked like rolling hills of rubble scattered with cranes, grapplers, and firefighters. The excavation had an eerie hum coming from the darkness and dust.

I walked slowly into the Pit, to a stretcher where my brother's body was covered with an American flag.

Kevin had been found in the area of the North Tower, wearing his turnout coat emblazoned with his last name on the back. No doubt about his identity. Lying next to him was his eighteen-inch officer's tool, a special crowbar carried by lieutenants and captains.

Battalion Chief Bob Strong greeted me. We had been lieutenants together in Ladder 128 and in the same study group for promotions. It was good to see a familiar face. I bent down to peel back the flag and look at my brother's face one last time. I felt Bob's hand on my shoulder.

"I don't think you want to do that," he said. Bob was right. Kevin's body had suffered terrible injuries and five months of decay. I didn't want that image to be the lasting memory of my brother.

Engine 33 had been called to respond to the Pile as well. As we gathered around the stretcher, all the heavy equipment shut down. Silence covered the Pile as we bent down to grasp the stretcher. I was at the head of the stretcher on the right, leading my brother home.

We walked through Ground Zero on a dusty dirt road and then up a ramp from the dark, cold pit, south toward Liberty Street. First responders and construction workers stopped their work and lined the ramp to salute or otherwise show respect. Engine 33 and I walked from the B stairs in the collapsed North Tower where we found Kevin, then past the ruins of the South Tower. In my turnout gear and white helmet, I felt the sadness of carrying my brother and the weight of command.

We loaded the stretcher into the ambulance, and I sat in the back with my brother. It reminded me of the times we used to ride in the back of the ambulance together as EMTs in the Rockaway Point Volunteer Fire Department. Kevin had been a teenager then. He'd died at age forty-two.

A police escort led the ambulance to the morgue at Bellevue Hospital as Engine 33 followed behind, its red emergency lights flashing. It was a bit spooky that we were going to Bellevue, since my brother had worked there as a paramedic before he came into the FDNY.

The ride to the morgue was the saddest time in my life. Tears streamed down my face as I laid my hand on my brother's shoulder, totally overcome with grief. Through the rear window of the ambulance, I saw the lights of Engine 33, a reminder of how Kevin loved the FDNY and his firehouse. I wondered how I was going to be able to escort him into the morgue without breaking down.

I remembered being sworn in as a New York City firefighter in front of City Hall by Mayor Koch in 1981. I was given a badge in the traditional FDNY shape of a Maltese cross. The badge number was 1513, which to me had great significance. It was one of my favorite Gospel readings, John 15:13: "There is no greater love than to lay down one's life for a friend."

I wore that badge until I was promoted to lieutenant. When my brother Kevin became a firefighter, I arranged for him to have my old firefighter badge, 1513.

Suddenly, in the back of the ambulance, calm washed over me. I thought of all the times Kevin and I had sailed in Jamaica Bay on his eighteen-foot Hobie Cat sailboat. Life was so simple and filled with joy then, and we would fly one pontoon hull in swift winds. I almost felt the warm winds of sailing with my brother fill the back of the ambulance. My brother was home in my heart with my memories of sailing.

Now that Kevin had been found, we could have a proper funeral. On February 10, 2002, newly elected Mayor Mike Bloomberg attended my brother's funeral at St. Margaret's Roman Catholic Church, the first of many such services he would attend.

"I did not know your son," Mayor Bloomberg told my parents. He referenced the motto on the face of the church, "Serving God and the Community Since 1860," drawing a parallel to the sacrifice Kevin and all the firefighters had made. "On behalf of all the people of New York City, all we can say is thank you for giving us Kevin."

I followed Bloomberg and thanked the mayor.

"Your presence here and your support means a lot to us, my family, and the Fire Department," I said. I was glad he'd chosen to attend Kevin's funeral, both for my family's sake and for the morale of the department and the city.

In my eulogy, I talked about how much Kevin loved his family and his FDNY family. Then I told the story of our last ambulance ride to Bellevue and how I'd turned my grief into good memories with Kevin.

Several of Kevin's friends and the officers of Engine 33 spoke. As the funeral ended, his FDNY brothers carried Kevin's flag-wrapped casket through the church's doors and hoisted it onto the top of an FDNY engine. My family and I walked behind the rig, followed by members of

Engine 33 and flanked by marching firefighters and the Emerald Society band. The bagpipes and muffled drums played "Amazing Grace" as we moved slowly down 80th Street to St. John Cemetery, a one-block walk. Along the route was a line of thousands of saluting firefighters in uniform.

As we walked, I thought of the last time I saw my brother's face. He had been so calm as he turned to lead his firefighters up the B staircase.

16

———

THROUGH THE LENS

THE FILM BY Jules and Gédéon Naudet, simply named *9/11*, aired on Sunday evening, March 10, 2002, on CBS. In addition to the footage they'd shot that day, the Naudet brothers had filmed an additional 140 hours of reportage and interviews of firefighters.

When the Naudets had started their probie project, no producer or distributor was particularly interested. Suddenly they had a hot property.

But they were exhausted as well. Jules and Gédéon spent ten days with their parents, who had moved to Los Angeles, to think about their next steps. They looked at every frame of film and thought about how they wanted to tell the story.

"It was an important thing for the Fire Department," Jules said, "showing their bravery and selflessness and heroism."

"For me, it was never like history has chosen us to tell the story," Gédéon said. "It was much simpler. How do we honor the incredible work, heroism, and sacrifice of those guys we started to know?" But, in fact, history chose each of us that day. As Jules puts it, "There is always a witness for history."

Most producers just wanted to buy their footage. But the Naudets wanted control of how the firehouse and department were portrayed.

"It was about our brothers, something to show humanity and to show hope, despite the senseless killing," Jules said. "We wanted to show that, when it's important, New York City locks elbows and pulls together."

The Naudets ended up making a deal with CBS. They were teamed up with award-winning journalist and news producer Susan Zirinsky, then the executive producer of the show *48 Hours* (who later would become the first woman president of CBS News), whom Jules calls their "amazing fairy godmother."

They started meeting with CBS editors at the beginning of January. But they had more groundwork to do. The attacks had devastated the FDNY and the brothers wanted to show the survivors and family members that their stories would be treated with respect. Jules had caught the last earthly glimpses of dozens of firefighters who had gathered in the North Tower lobby, about to ascend the stairs to do their jobs. They wanted grieving families to have the snippets of tape showing those last sacred moments.

The guys in the Duane Street firehouse knew the names of some, and others could be identified by their unit numbers. They painstakingly combed through the footage, and, with the help of James Hanlon, who went around to various firehouses with the pictures, they identified sixty-nine of FDNY's bravest who had been captured on tape for at least a few seconds. Then they invited their loved ones to view the piece of film.

Initially, many of the family members were against the project. Rumors were flying that the footage was gruesome, that they had "filmed carnage and body parts and people dying in front of the camera," Gédéon told the BBC. "So, everyone was very much afraid of what they were expecting to see."

But none of that was true. Perhaps in reaction to their own trauma, both Jules and Gédéon had gone into a sort of self-censorship mode. "We never filmed anybody dying or dead in front of us," Jules said. "We always refused." In the end, nothing they'd shot was so gruesome they couldn't include it in their film.

About two weeks before the documentary was scheduled to be broadcast, they held a two-hour meeting at the fire academy, set up by the FDNY and the unions. The rumors had riled emotions; people were screaming at Jules and Gédéon. They finally had to stop the group meeting and talked to each family member, one by one, showing them the tape of their loved one.

People began to understand that it was their desire to honor the firefighters' memory. In gratitude for the department's help, the Naudets arranged with the FDNY union to set up an education fund for firefighters, spouses, and children from the proceeds of the film. (Over twenty years, they would substantially contribute to and raise $52 million for scholarships.)

For months, the brothers had been watching the tapes, "hearts bleeding, admiring their heroes," as Jules put it. The CBS team of editors had embraced the project, feeling their work would be a consecration to those who'd died, to all New Yorkers and the entire country—to all those who had felt helpless that day.

Mayor Giuliani had demanded to see it first, but CBS and the Naudets refused. He'd see it along with the rest of New York. Very few images had leaked out. I had seen only a few clips. "Their footage—which includes the only visual documentation of the event from beginning to end—is the true Zapruder film of the New York terror attacks," wrote their friend and coproducer David Friend in *Vanity Fair*.

Producer Zirinsky arranged for the film to be broadcast with none of the firefighters' rough language bleeped out and uninterrupted by commercials—though there were three short public service announcements—which made for two very intense hours.

That evening in March 2002, thousands of New Yorkers crowded into bars and restaurants with televisions, wanting to be with others as they experienced that horrible day, this time from inside the North Tower. Few wanted to be alone.

The Naudets watched the documentary with their parents. I watched it at home with Ginny, Christine, and Gregory.

I had not shared a lot of details of my experience with Ginny and the kids. The film took everyone, including my family, inside the World Trade Center. We sat in our living room as the narrative played out almost in real time, those 102 minutes from the first plane hitting the North Tower to its collapse and me jumping on top of Jules. Inches, moments, small decisions—do I go left or right?—made a difference in who lived and who died.

The documentary was followed by emotional interviews of the guys of Engine 7 and Ladder 1: Captain Tardio, Lieutenant Walsh, Firefighters O'Neill, Braithwaite, Van Cleaf, and the rest, including me. The stories of their experiences that day took viewers not just into the tower but into their hearts and minds. The project had started as a film about a probie, but it had become a story about the firehouse and the bravery of firefighters.

Watching from my couch was surreal, like entering a big flashback, a bad dream that I knew was real. I saw myself inside the lobby talking on the radio, sending firefighters up, and, movingly, seeing my brother taking his firefighters upstairs for the last time.

"I remember walking down West Street," I said on camera. "I just remember how much my brother and I used to love being downtown, and doing this job. And how now I didn't love it anymore."

I'd told that to Jules in September, only two weeks after the attacks, when he interviewed me. I had meant it. But moving through the grief and realizing that we could effect change—that I could be part of something bigger than myself—had by now given me a shred of hope that I would find my post-9/11 compass.

The documentary ended by showing photographs of every dead and missing member of the FDNY—343 men, arranged in groups of four—to the haunting song "Danny Boy," sung by Ronan Tynan, in homage to those ordinary heroes. It was a moving and powerful tribute, emphasizing the tremendous loss we as family members had suffered.

Some firefighters had a hard time watching it. Steve Olsen was in Orlando at Disney World when it aired. Halfway through watching it in a hotel room with his family, Olsen had to leave. He went outside and took a walk. It was too painful. A week later, he was back working at Ground Zero.

Many firefighters seen in the footage would never be found, but the film will for generations be a witness to the history of their bravery and sacrifice.

Over twenty years, almost a billion people would see the documentary. One of those people was Jake Knight, a young teenager from New Zealand being treated for acute myeloid leukemia, a rapidly spreading form of cancer. During six months in the hospital's isolation ward, he felt helpless. "The only thing that gave me strength and hope during that time was a documentary, *9/11*," he said. "I would watch it at least once a week. If the firefighters could deal with 9/11, I can deal with my sickness."

After Jake gained his strength back, Make-A-Wish Foundation granted him his wish to visit the FDNY and meet me. Jake and his mom flew to New York City, where we met at FDNY's headquarters and made him an Honorary Firefighter. As soon as we started talking, we had this sense that both of us had gone through something tough. From that moment, we became lifelong friends. The film *9/11* gave Jake the courage to get through treatments, and we at the FDNY inspired him to be a firefighter, which is his dream.

17

EMERGING FROM THE ASHES

T HE AIRING OF THE *9/11* documentary told our story from inside the World Trade Center and showed the guys from Engine 7 and Ladder 1 emotionally returning to the Duane Street firehouse. Covered with dust, glassy-eyed firefighters hugged each other as they stood on the apparatus floor, now empty of rigs that had earlier been crushed by the falling high-rise buildings. Upon learning that everyone from the firehouse was alive, we watched Captain Tardio from Engine 7 say what we all were wondering: "How did we make it out of there?"

After the film appeared, New Yorkers again made a point of knocking on firehouses' doors to say thank you.

Some teenagers from a nearby high school came to visit Duane Street on their own to meet the firefighters of "Miracle House." Very touched by the movie, they shook firefighters' hands, checked out the apparatus, then asked the guy on housewatch, "Can we meet the chief?"

Duane Street was still split in two: the WTC Incident Command took up one half, and Engine 7, Ladder 1, and Battalion 1, the other. I was in my office on the second floor, above the apparatus bay. When the housewatch called, my aide picked it up. "A bunch of kids want to see you," he said. "Can the chief come down?"

"Sure," I said. For years, I'd talked to kids about fire safety.

A half dozen excited teenagers milled around on the apparatus floor, checking out our replacement engine, ladder, and battalion SUV, chatting with firefighters in uniform. The teens looked at me with recognition, and a bit of awe, even though I wasn't wearing my bunker gear and helmet.

I shook hands with each one of them, and then one girl piped up. "I thought you were taller," she said. I laughed. It was clear she perceived firefighters as bigger than life, almost like superheroes. Maybe today, she saw her heroes as more ordinary, someone she could become.

The appreciation from the community was gratifying. But for firefighters inside Duane Street—and in firehouses all over the city—the sheer numbers of those lost were overwhelming. Firefighters felt a sense of camaraderie as they continued to do normal runs, but the trauma remained.

Added to the angst was the nine-month recovery period of searching for bodies or body parts of the deceased so that families could hold a funeral. Those who discovered human remains experienced a sense of mission accomplished, yet what they saw was more than anyone should see, especially as bodies started to decay. Some perhaps shuddered to think how close they'd come to the same fate.

After many months, some families resigned themselves to the fact that their loved ones might never be found, so they settled for a memorial service. When remains were found, they held a funeral. This meant that the FDNY had more than 343 services for those lost.

The FDNY had to figure out how to take care of its members'

mental health and, at the same time, continue recovery operations on the Pile and the normal FDNY functions to save life and property.

Trauma and grief were not the only reasons firefighters sought counseling. After 9/11, the job and the firehouse went through rapid change. Many, like Captain Tardio with twenty years of service, were considering retirement. Others perhaps left the job in response to their families' fears for their safety. Others stayed but were promoted more quickly than they might have been, with new responsibilities. New firefighters were coming in. The constant shifts in the firehouse family brought new stresses. Nothing seemed to be the same anymore.

Constant news coverage of the attacks and new threats of terrorism compounded firehouses' stress.

In my firehouse, some firefighters felt the tension between belonging to a "miracle" firehouse, which had been spared, and "survivor guilt" over being so lucky. Being called heroes was for those who had made the supreme sacrifice; we were just ordinary people searching for a new normal.

"I'm not any better than anybody else," O'Neill said. "I'm just a firefighter. In a way, I feel that there must be a reason. And it's scary to think what the hell the reason might be. What reason—what lies in my future?"

One firefighter quietly confided to his captain one night that he didn't want to be alive.

"I don't want to go kill myself," he said. "I just don't want to be alive right now. I don't understand what that means."

The captain empathized with the firefighter's feeling. The two men talked about survivor's guilt, and the captain urged him to seek counseling. The firefighter agreed.

For me, the concern was how we would manage the next extreme terrorist attack on skyscrapers. I also was worried about my firefighters and the pressures they were under, with both their physical and mental health. I talked to the captains to make sure they were looking after their guys and the officers. I told them, "Call me anytime you need help."

THE FDNY's COUNSELING SERVICE UNIT (CSU), a small unit located in SoHo, a mile and a half from the World Trade Center, was first created to take care of firefighters with alcohol or substance abuse. In the 1980s, it expanded to care for firehouses with a line-of-duty death or those units that responded to a tragic fire with multiple deaths, especially those of children.

After a tragedy, a professional counselor with a peer counselor, usually a trained fire officer, would hold a Critical Incident Stress Debriefing (CISD) with firehouse members. With my graduate education in counseling and after attending several CISD courses, I had become one of those peer counselors a decade before 9/11.

In these group settings, firefighters told their accounts of fatal fires. The professional clinician conducted a group session in the firehouse. Peer counselors listened empathetically to each firefighter's story to ensure that no one felt isolated. The session ended with information about PTSD and additional mental health resources.

With the collapse of the WTC towers, the CSU immediately shifted into high gear. The old one-to-one or small-group counseling models in a handful of firehouses would not be enough. Working with key professionals, Malachy Corrigan, the director of CSU since 1982, developed a crisis counseling plan to care for the mental health of more than 15,000 firefighters, EMS, dispatchers, and civilian personnel.

One of the most innovative services used in the aftermath of 9/11 was the Firehouse Clinician Program. Built upon Malachy's firehouse counseling model, the program was expanded to forty-two firehouses hit hard by the trauma of 9/11.

A professional counselor physically worked in the firehouse. They met with on-duty firefighters to listen and give them information about PTSD. The clinician pointed out that emotional reactions to the events of 9/11 were normal. They arranged opportunities for firefighters to tell stories of their experiences and about the friends they'd lost. At any time, a firefighter could walk up to the counselor to have a more personal conversation.

The counselor was not there to do psychotherapy in the firehouse; instead, they offered an empathic ear, made mental health services accessible, matched services to the needs of the firehouse, and identified individuals who were feeling depressed or isolated.

To accomplish these goals, the clinician first had to build trust among the firefighters, which started with the captain. If the clinician had the captain's confidence, firefighters would follow suit. When I ran into the clinician walking around the Duane Street firehouse, I made a point to say hello as a sign of support for the program. But at the same time, I knew that she was there for the firefighters. As during fires, there are times when the chief needs to get out of the way.

According to CSU, crisis counseling is about relocating memories of the deceased from your head to your heart. After building trust, firefighters often would point to pictures on the wall of fallen firefighters and tell firehouse stories about the person. It was a way of keeping good memories alive.

The healing power of groups and storytelling fits nicely into firehouse culture. However, when people were on duty, the clinician had to walk a tightrope of encouraging storytelling without opening the floodgates of emotions.

Every thirty days, we rotated six hundred firefighters to the World Trade Center Task Force for recovery operations. This group was separate from the rest of the job with a different work schedule. At the end of each thirty-day detail, we required everyone to attend a debrief that provided information on PTSD and destigmatized counseling services. We could mandate debriefings, but we could not order counseling; instead, we made it welcoming and easy to attain.

With more than seventy members of the FDNY losing a father, brother, or son, CSU created special group sessions. In October, CSU asked me to attend a session with a group of firefighters who had lost a brother. I was to be part of the group and not a peer counselor.

However, during these sessions, as firefighters started to tell their emotional stories, I slipped into the familiar role of peer counselor. I understood their pain and compassionately mirrored back what they were saying. I answered any questions they had about that day, especially if I had seen their brother.

By the end of the second session, people were grateful that I was part of the group, but I felt exhausted. The group did not relieve my stress but instead intensified my overloaded emotions, commonly known as "compassion fatigue." I was using my emotional energy to worry about the guys losing their brothers. I, too, had lost my brother. But my capacity for playing both roles—chief and counselor—was being stretched to its limit. I quietly backed out of the brothers' group. I was learning to know the limits of my ability to help others.

To normalize the benefit of counseling, Chief Hayden and I did a short videotape about the importance of counseling services. This tape went to every firehouse and EMS station. By this time, firefighters recognized and trusted us, which we used to reinforce that it was okay to have strong feelings about losing friends and the changing post-9/11 world. We emphasized that counseling was just another tool to manage post-traumatic stress.

Between September 2001 and June 2005, CSU provided direct counseling services to over 7,100 active-duty members and 500 retired members. In 2002 alone, CSU counseled nearly 2,900 active-duty members. Many in the FDNY took advantage of services for themselves and their family members.

Despite the resources, some firefighters continued to suffer for years. People who retired within the next year or so often regretted it; they no longer had the firehouse and the people who understood their experiences.

Many firefighters struggled with memories triggered by odors, sounds, the sight of an airplane against a blue sky, the numbers 911 and 343. They wrestled with insomnia and nightmares. Some avoided lower Manhattan. A few firefighters turned to drugs and alcohol, even lost their jobs and their marriages.

"I'm not on the fire department no more because of 9/11," one firefighter told an interviewer ten years after the event. "Not married no more because of 9/11."

Post-traumatic stress was part of the 9/11 experience. Fortunately, most firefighters did not develop debilitating long-term PTSD, thanks in large part to being able to share their stories and their connection with each other and CSU.

RECOVERING FROM TRAUMA requires turning memories into new dreams by connecting to others, reflecting on the past, envisioning the future, and enhancing the present with a new purpose. This sounds theoretical, but I discovered this process during my own journey of finding resilience and watching the FDNY, little by little, bounce back.

In the firehouses, the increased intensity of connecting was more apparent. Firefighters gathered in the kitchen, TV room, or apparatus floor just to be with each other. Almost every firefighter Jules interviewed said that the firehouse was the most comfortable place to be after 9/11. They did not have to explain what they did or how they were feeling. Everyone knew each other's story and understood their experience.

Like me, firefighters felt the need to protect their families from the horrific details of that day. Yet the memory and emotions could not be kept bottled up inside. The firehouse became a place sometimes to vent, but mostly simply a place to be understood.

The firefighters' families were a different story. Those who'd lost a spouse, parent, sibling, child, or friend also went through the trauma process. Though firefighters tried to be there for those who had lost a family member, many houses were overwhelmed with losses.

Ginny's post-9/11 journey to resilience mainly focused on our children and their routines—their schoolwork and swim practices with weekend swim meets. There was the hope of doing well in school and swimming and a vision for college. Getting Christine and Gregory to work hard and look toward the future took some of the pain away from losing their uncle. Ginny also made time for small things that gave her comfort and pleasure: reading novels, sewing, taking walks. On the anniversaries of 9/11, Ginny and I always take a long walk on the beach, quietly remembering how lucky we are to have each other.

But she had to change some habits. Ginny had relished reading the *New York Times* front to back each day. But the paper's continuous news coverage of 9/11's aftermath prompted her to suspend that practice for a while. She had to draw the line to avoid the constant reminders about the day she'd almost become a widow.

Eventually, like me, she sought a new purpose in her career, obtaining a Wound, Ostomy, and Continence Nursing Certification, recognizing her skills in a specialized nursing field. This is a demanding job where nurses take care of patients' surgical wounds, pressure ulcers, and ostomy appliances for bodily functions. Of course, all these stories would come out at the kitchen table, which would quickly ruin my appetite. But, as Ginny put it, her work allowed patients to go home to live everyday life with their families. Her new purpose gave others hope. She eventually got back to reading the *New York Times* and is one of the few people I know who can complete its crossword puzzle.

Like Ginny, who had believed for a time that I had died, many significant others of surviving firefighters were glad not to have their stories in the public eye, but they hated that others did not recognize the pain they went through that day. The CSU provided counseling, giving these families a place to tell their stories and move beyond the grief.

Moving beyond grief sometimes meant becoming even closer to the firehouse. There are many stories of how children whose firefighter parents died have grown up to be amazing young adults. Some became "legacy firefighters," men and women who joined the FDNY after a family member died in the line of duty. In one class of three hundred probationary firefighters, there were twenty-one legacy firefighters. Their family sacrifice became part of the new firefighter's identity and purpose.

ON MAY 30, 2002, we reached the bottom of Ground Zero, eight months and nineteen days after the Twin Towers collapsed. The "Pile," now the "Pit," had been swept clean. We had removed 108,342 truckloads of rubble. Human remains had been found all over the site. A map with red dots marking each retrieval showed people inside and outside the buildings' original footprints. Little decisions had made the difference between life and death. If I had gone south when I came out of the tower instead of north, I would not have survived.

Of those firefighters who died, bodies of fewer than half had been recovered. A stretcher, bearing only an American flag, was placed in the center of the ramp at the lowest point of the Pit to represent all the victims who died that day.

At exactly 10:28 a.m., the time the second tower fell, a series of five clangs of the fire bell, repeated four times, broke the stillness of Ground Zero. Since 1870, the code 5-5-5-5 has signaled the line-of-duty death of a firefighter.

As thousands of observers stood in silence, many with tears streaming down their faces, I placed one hand on the front right side of the stretcher. To my left was the FDNY's EMS Division Chief Charlie Wells. Behind us were two officers from the Port Authority Police and two NYPD officers. Several of us carrying the stretcher had lost brothers. We lifted the stretcher and then, in unison, slowly walked up the long ramp, just as I had carried my brother out earlier in February. I felt a sense of calmness as we supported each other on the journey out of the Pit. We had endured so much, yet there was still a lot of work to do to prepare for the next disaster.

Lining the path out of the Pit was an honor guard of first responders in dress uniform and others who had been part of the rescue and recovery operations for the last nine months. We were holding a stretcher that represented all those who died at the World Trade Center. Fathers, mothers, husbands, wives, partners, brothers, sisters, sons, daughters, friends. We placed the stretcher into a waiting ambulance as if recovering the body of a loved one.

Two buglers, one from the FDNY and one from the NYPD, played taps, followed by an NYPD helicopter flyover. Our symbolic walk was a way to honor the victims and heroes who we lost.

The last piece of steel, a fifty-ton column with first responders' messages painted on it, was lifted onto a flatbed truck, covered in black cloth, and driven up the extended ramp. It was a symbol that the recovery and dismantling of twisted steel were concluded. This piece of steel now stands upright in the 9/11 Memorial Museum, where my white battalion chief's helmet and Jules's camera are displayed in a glass case.

The closing of the site was the end of a nine-month operation of digging and searching. We were relieved that it came to an end, yet disappointed that we had not recovered more people. Carrying the stretcher up from six stories below grade was taking the first step away from the ashes and horror.

During the first week of June, the FDNY usually holds its annual Medal Day ceremony on the steps of City Hall, honoring the heroic acts of bravery and initiative by firefighters and EMS. This year was different. At a meeting at headquarters, I asked the fire commissioner and senior chiefs, "How can we award medals of courage to anyone but the 343 who gave their lives on that September morning?" We agreed that, while there were many brave acts that day, the medals belonged to our firefighters, fire marshal, and paramedics who had made the supreme sacrifice. FDNY's Medal Day ceremony was suspended for 2002.

But medals and their accompanying ribbon for the dress uniform are part of the Fire Department's tradition. They recognize courage during dangerous times. I proposed that everyone in the Fire Department who responded to the World Trade Center attacks be given a medal with the image of firefighters raising the American flag at Ground Zero on the front and the FDNY logo on the back. The corresponding one-inch ribbon, half purple and half black—the colors of our mourning bunting—would have the number "343" embossed in gold on the purple background.

The medal recognized three different types of valor. The survivor medal and ribbon with two stars were given to those at the WTC before the buildings collapsed. The rescuer medal and ribbon with one star were for those who responded after 10:28 but before the collapse of WTC-7 at 5:20 p.m. And the campaign award was for members who worked at Ground Zero after the collapse of WTC-7 until the closing of the site on May 30, 2002.

At first, firefighters and senior chiefs objected to this idea. "We don't need any medals! We know what we did that day. And medals are for those who died trying to save others."

"The medals and ribbons are for your families, your kids, and grand-children," I said. "They are to be handed down generation to generation." After some convincing, we distributed the set of medals and ribbons to our members. Today, the ribbon is worn proudly on the dress uniform and is considered by firefighters to be their highest award. New firefighters, seeing their peers with the survivor ribbon, wonder what it must have been like that day.

TWO DAYS AFTER THE LAST piece of steel was removed from Ground Zero, the Duane Street firehouse celebrated a different kind of ritual. On June 1, 2002, Jules Naudet married his fiancée, Jacqueline Longa, a human resources counselor from Brooklyn. The wedding ceremony was held at our almost century-old firehouse on Duane Street.

The firehouse wedding took place on the apparatus floor, where we held meetings for the WTC recovery operation. Jacqueline wore a beautiful white wedding dress and veil; Jules wore a tuxedo. Fifty-five firefighters, with their wives and girlfriends, were in attendance. Gédéon was the best man. I gave them a special "Firehouse Blessing," reminding the lovely couple of the importance of staying close to each other during difficult times, and if they ever needed anything, they now had fifty-five brothers and forever will be part of the FDNY family. Jacqueline and Jules looked at each other with glowing happiness as they made their sacred vows. Already they had been through good times and bad, but they could only envision a good life together.

In the middle of the ritual, you could feel the firehouse suddenly transformed from a place of fatigue to one of hope and joy. At the end of the ceremony, firefighters threw rose petals from their helmets and sprayed fire extinguishers.

The reception was at the historic old civic building near City Hall. The newlyweds rode the few blocks in the chief's car, Jules's last official FDNY ride. (I think Jacqueline was too nervous for Jules and me to ever respond to another fire together.) During the reception, firefighters danced their hearts out, purging nine months of emotions.

After midnight, Jules and his lovely bride returned to the firehouse. In the kitchen, where so much had taken place over the previous year, they ate a piece of wedding cake.

"This has been a place of sorrow, of loss, of tears," Jules said. "But we were replacing the bunting of sorrow with beautiful things." The newlyweds stayed up so late they missed the flight for their honeymoon the next day. For them, for all of us who survived, life would be forever different, but on this day, we celebrated. We had experienced a great tragedy, but people would find love, get married, have children, and live their lives with hope for the future.

18

HOW CAN I HELP?

A FTER KEVIN'S FUNERAL IN FEBRUARY, all I wanted to do was get back to normal—whatever that was. What could be so hard about that? Ginny was worried about my long hours. Before 9/11, I'd worked two twenty-four-hour tours a week with lots of family time in between. After the attacks, I was working seven days a week. So I cherished normalcy and wanted to go back to a predictable schedule and do activities with the kids.

But I also wanted to help shape the future of the FDNY. Based on my experience on 9/11 and recovery operations at Ground Zero, I had an innate sense of what we needed to do. And then I got an unexpected opportunity.

At the beginning of March 2002, Chief Pete Hayden and I were summoned to FDNY headquarters to meet with new Fire Commissioner Nicholas Scoppetta, who was a top-notch reformer, ranging from his work on the Knapp Commission in the 1970s to heading up the Administration for Children's Services in the 1990s. He introduced us to consultants from McKinsey & Company. The commissioner asked us to work with McKinsey, which donated its services to New York City to write separate reports for the FDNY and NYPD about the response to 9/11 and what to do differently in the future. Pete and I agreed to help. It was meant to be a short, three-week detail. Instead, our work with McKinsey took five intense months.

McKinsey senior partner Carlos Kershner oversaw the core team of Lisa Frazier, Caroline Gaffney, Yakov Kofner, Gregory Parsons, Lee Miles III, and other support staff.

In the FDNY, we pulled in EMS Division Chiefs John Peruggia and Walter Kowalczyk, Chief of Staff Mike Vecchi, along with many others on a part-time basis. But it was Hayden and I who worked every weekday as part of the core McKinsey team, often serving as interpreters of firefighting expressions and procedures.

I also worked a fifteen-hour night tour or an occasional twenty-four-hour tour once a week in the firehouse. Early on, Chief Sal Cassano told me, "Joe, you are detailed to the McKinsey project, so you don't have to work in the field."

He was trying to ease my burden, and I appreciated that. But I needed to be in the firehouse to remain connected to the firefighters. An eighty-hour workweek became my new routine. Ginny was not thrilled but knew I was trying to navigate this new reality.

Hayden and I had known each other for a long time. Pete, about ten years older than me, was considered a "driver." Give him something, and he'd run with it and don't get in his way. My role was more analytical, aimed at strategic thinking. Together, we made a good team. For a while, we shared an office. Of course, he had the bigger desk; rank has its privileges. And we had the shared experience of being in command in the North Tower. Both of us were motivated to move beyond the ashes, both personally and as a department.

At headquarters, we took over a conference room and equipped an office to review audio transmissions from 911 operators and fire dispatchers, as well as the film shot by Jules and Gédéon. We did hundreds of hours of individual interviews with firefighters and EMTs who'd responded to the 9/11 attacks and barely escaped with their lives. Everything was very raw. Listening to tapes from civilians who'd died was particularly wrenching, as callers told dispatchers, "It's so hot, I'm burning up. I'm going to die."

Among those tapes we eventually listened to were transmissions of Battalion 7 Chief Orio Palmer and his men inside the South Tower. They had taken an elevator to the 41st floor, halfway to the impact zone, which stretched from the 78th to the 84th floors. Extremely fit, Palmer made it to the 78th floor. "Numerous 10-45s, Code 1," Palmer said, using the FDNY radio term for dead people. He saw a couple of pockets of fire and called for Engine companies to tackle them and Ladder companies for search and rescue. I was in awe of his determination and calm, decisive tone. It was tough to hear Palmer speaking to Lieutenant Joe Leavey from Ladder 15, who I had worked with for years. Under extreme conditions and only minutes before the collapse, Orio and Joe, with firefighters from Ladder 15 and other units, ran up three dozen flights of stairs to rescue those injured and trapped. It was their last act of bravery.

One of those with Palmer was Ronnie Bucca, the only FDNY fire marshal killed on 9/11. A former Green Beret and member of FDNY Rescue 1, Bucca had become famous in the FDNY after surviving a five-story fall from a tenement fire escape in the 1980s. Nicknamed the "Flying Fireman" after his miraculous escape from death, he returned to work after a year of physical rehabilitation. After the 1993 bombing of the WTC, he insisted that terrorists would return to finish the job, but his warning had made little impact. I wondered how he had felt when he realized that, tragically, he had been right.

After months of concentrated research, we knew more than anyone about what transpired that day. At times, I got frustrated.

"We know what happened," I said one day. "Let's get to what we are going to do about it for the future. How can we bring about change sitting in a conference room dwelling on the past?"

Lisa Frazier, a chemical engineer from Australia, took me aside and said, "Joe, we need to get all the facts before we make any recommendations. Trust me. We'll get there."

Lisa was not only smart, but she was also tough. She didn't take any guff from Pete or me. She heard some of the most traumatic stories and didn't flinch.

In early May, we split the team to learn how the rest of the country's fire departments handled major incidents like wildfires, tornados, and earthquakes.

Hayden went to the East Coast and the middle of the country. I went with Lisa and the other half of the team to the West Coast to visit departments in Phoenix, Los Angeles, San Francisco, and Seattle. The departments we visited were more than willing to help us, but they wanted to hear personal accounts.

I did my first 9/11 PowerPoint on the WTC with the Los Angeles City and County Fire Departments. I could feel the emotions in the room filled with dozens of seasoned fire chiefs who knew what leadership at a tragic fire scene meant.

As I explained how I ordered firefighters, including my brother, to evacuate and rescue those trapped, I looked over at Lisa. For the first time, this tough Australian woman had a tear running down her face. Her work was no longer a consulting project; it was personal.

We learned something new with every fire department we visited. The common thread reinforced the value of the Incident Management System and assigning an Incident Management Team (IMT) for large-scale events.

On the long flight home, feeling supported by our West Coast fire chiefs, I sat with Lisa on the plane.

"The commissioner is impressed with your work," Lisa told me, "and he likes your insight on how the FDNY needs to change."

Of course, I was thrilled. Then she told me something I had trouble comprehending.

"I think the commissioner wants you to come on staff," she said.

"Wait . . . what?" I said. I could not imagine jumping ranks so quickly, so I simply smiled and discounted the possibility.

On May 28, 2002, I was promoted from battalion chief to deputy chief, based on a civil service exam now-retired Chief Byrnes had urged me to take a couple of years earlier. Standing onstage in front of hundreds of people, including my family, I raised my right hand to take the oath of office. As Commissioner Scoppetta congratulated me, he asked me to come on board as a staff chief. A staff chief position is usually for people having more than thirty years' seniority. I didn't even have twenty-one years on the job. He was asking me to go from having gold oak leaves on the collar to a two-star chief, virtually skipping the deputy chief rank with eagles on my collar.

Stunned, I replied, "I can't. I need more experience." The commissioner just smiled.

All night I thought about what the commissioner was asking me to do. I had survived 9/11 and worked endless hours on understanding how the FDNY needed to change.

Part of resilience is shouldering the burden of knowledge to make a difference. The next day, I went back to Scoppetta and said, "How can I help?"

The final FDNY-McKinsey Report, titled *Increasing FDNY's Preparedness*, was published on August 19, 2002. The 169-page document examined the moment-by-moment response of the FDNY on 9/11. We were radically honest about everything, from a lack of interagency incident command and information sharing to inadequate technology and outdated procedures.

The report recommended a plan for implementing FDNY changes in operational preparedness, planning and management, communications and technology, and family and member support. Its conclusions and recommendations would also play a significant role in influencing the 9/11 Commission.

A week later, I raised my right hand again, and along with six other deputy chiefs, was promoted to a two-star deputy assistant chief. Little did I know that Commissioner Scoppetta would mentor me as a young leader through our many conversations, demanding excellence in everything and sending me for graduate degrees at the Naval Postgraduate School and the Harvard Kennedy School.

Scoppetta acted swiftly on the McKinsey recommendations and instituted a new borough command structure. He appointed me as the chief for planning and strategy. Scoppetta then instructed Hayden and me to form work groups to implement the rest of the McKinsey recommendations.

For almost 140 years, the FDNY had worried only about the day-to-day operations of putting out fires. After the tragic morning of September 11, our world had become more complex, and the FDNY, in turn, had to adapt. I would play a foremost role in making these recommendations a reality, designing the new Fire Department Operations Center (FDOC) and writing the first strategic plan in the FDNY's long history.

The strategic plan compelled the department to envision the future by enhancing emergency response operations, management, and diversity, as well as technology, health, and safety. We outlined twenty priority objectives, including enhancing our special operations units and designing new fireboats. Scoppetta said that he "considered the strategic plan one of the most important documents FDNY has ever produced." This was an opportunity to turn the pain of 9/11 into a new purpose.

FOR A YEAR, members of the FDNY had been going to endless wakes, funerals, and memorial services. I had attended dozens. But we still needed closure. After the WTC site had been closed in May, I approached the fire commissioner and senior leadership to mention this concern.

I had suggested that we conduct one large memorial service for the entire FDNY, a way to honor those we had lost together. The commissioner agreed. On October 12, 2002, after most of the individual funerals had occurred and after the first anniversary of the event, we held the FDNY memorial at Madison Square Garden.

The last time I had been in Madison Square Garden was on October 20, 2001, to attend the "Concert for New York City." I brought my fifteen-year-old daughter Christine. It seemed like the history of rock-and-roll all showed up for one concert to bring hope to the victims of 9/11. Organized by Paul McCartney, it included sixty artists, like The Who, David Bowie, Elton John, Eric Clapton, the Rolling Stones, Bon Jovi, Jay-Z, Destiny's Child, the Backstreet Boys, James Taylor, Billy Joel, Melissa Etheridge, to name a few. Every song was so emotional and uplifting that it felt like a concert finale.

I was delighted to take my daughter to the best concert of our lives. After a month of sadness, Christine was smiling to be with me during a pretty cool concert for a teenager. The outpouring of the artists' love made it a fantastic night to escape the reality of that day for six hours of performances and music.

Toward the end of the concert, Firefighter Mike Moran spoke to the audience, explaining that his brother, Battalion Chief John Moran, was killed on 9/11. John and I had been firefighters together. Mike ended his remarks by saying, "In the spirit of the Irish people, Osama bin Laden, you can kiss my royal Irish ass!" The audience erupted in loud applause.

A year later, the mood was more somber. It was a rainy fall day, as if the heavens were crying with us. We packed 19,000 people into Madison Square Garden, with tens of thousands of firefighters from departments around the world lining New York's streets. Millions of people watched on TV.

For several hours, we listened to music, heard messages of hope from religious leaders of every faith. The names of our fallen brothers were read as their photos flashed on big screens. Each of their families received a polished wooden case with four medals, including the FDNY Medal of Valor, presented by white-gloved firefighters.

We received condolences from political leaders. Mayor Bloomberg spoke, followed by former Mayor Giuliani. As Giuliani concluded his remarks, he said, "Let's give all our heroes a round of applause."

The arena erupted in a standing ovation that got louder and louder, lasting for over ten minutes. This was not merely a way to honor those who had sacrificed their lives; it was a catharsis of emotion for everyone in the arena. The applause continued in the street. We released that pain as we remembered our fallen heroes.

19

IGNITING CHANGE

I F I AM GOING TO order firefighters into danger, they must be well equipped and prepared. I vividly remember an experience commanding at a third-alarm fire in the Bronx when a firefighter with maybe seven years on the job ran up to me.

"Hey, Chief, I'd like to talk to you," he said.

"Of course," I said.

He looked me in the eye and said, "Chief, I want to let you know that I will follow you down any hallway." Those words meant a lot to me, and I thanked him. The hallway at a fire is one of the most dangerous places to be. It acts as a chimney, with smoke and heat concentrated in a narrow area—indeed, a hazardous location to get through. For a firefighter to have the confidence to follow me into danger is the highest possible compliment any fire chief can receive. It is also a tremendous responsibility. It could mean the difference between life and death.

I felt that burden in September 2002 when, as a newly minted two-star chief, I began tackling my job implementing the radical changes facing the FDNY. We had to imagine better ways of managing large-scale events and getting agencies to work with each other while under extreme stress.

Frank Cruthers had replaced Dan Nigro as the chief of department. Cassano continued as chief of operations, with Hayden as the assistant chief of operations. We held several meetings with deputy commissioners and senior staff. People were anxious to cooperate but had no idea how to begin. Nor did I. But I started knocking on doors, having quiet conversations with my colleagues about what they saw as potential challenges and changes in their command.

Though some chiefs remained tentative, the chief of special operations, Michael Weinlein, seized the opportunity. The division had lost experienced members of the Rescue, Squad, and Hazmat units, and they had to rebuild at the same time they were responding to biohazard threats.

My own tasks—developing counterterrorism response plans, designing the Fire Department Operations Center, pushing for an urban Incident Management Team, finding new technologies for managing large fires, and writing the strategic plan—seemed immense. Not to mention responding to third alarms or greater when I had the Citywide Command. Then I got an unexpected visit from Firefighter Ray Pfeifer, whom I first met years ago when I was a covering captain for nine months in Engine 40.

His firehouse was one of the hardest hit. They had lost twelve men. I'd worked with most of these guys in Ray's firehouse, which was right next to Lincoln Center for the Performing Arts. There was no need to go to Lincoln Center for a show; there were plenty of characters in the firehouse, and Ray was on center stage.

After 9/11, Ray had worked down at Ground Zero nearly every day to recover the firefighters from his Engine 40 and Ladder 35 who were killed. Not only did Ray dig on the Pile, but he also took care of the families with young children. He was always upbeat, but I could tell something was bothering him.

"I love my firehouse, but there's too much grief," Ray said. "I need a change. Can I be your aide?"

I was delighted. I needed an aide, and Ray had excellent people skills. He became my driver, full-time aide, and confidant. Ray was always thinking of how he could make the job better. He could work a room, knew who to talk to and how to get things done, and always had his ear to the ground. When possible, he solved problems before they got to me. Ray was like the character Radar O'Reilly in the sitcom *M*A*S*H*; he knew what I thought before I told him.

We started throwing around leadership ideas when multiple agencies were involved and came up with some core principles of "connecting, collaborating, and coordinating." But we saw daily reminders of how people in various agencies, including the FDNY, tended to turn to their own group when under stress. It's human nature. I told Ray, "We'll have to work on breaking down these barriers one at a time."

The NYPD was creating a Counterterrorism Bureau with hundreds of officers. They attracted retired generals and other experienced people with impressive résumés to work for them. They expanded their presence at the FBI's Joint Terrorism Task Force (JTTF) and had a powerful voice in the mayor's office.

Scoppetta placed two of our fire marshals for the first time on the JTTF. But the FDNY's preparedness team had no big names or staff; it was just me. My knowledge of 9/11 and my work on the McKinsey Report gave me a unique perspective on preparedness. But, having worked in firehouses for most of my career, I was clueless when it came to headquarters and government politics.

Then Scoppetta brought in a young attorney, Kate Frucher. She had emerged from the subway into the chaos of lower Manhattan in the middle of the attacks and thus had a personal connection to events of that day. When Kate first told me that she was there at the moment the second plane hit the South Tower, I realized this was more than just a job for her.

While excited to join the FDNY, Kate admitted that she was no counterterrorism expert. But she knew how to get things done in government, having worked in the Clinton White House to help create the AmeriCorps national service program and previous government reform efforts in New York City. She had okay credentials, a bachelor's from Harvard and a law degree from Stanford.

At the time, the real threat from al-Qaeda and other terrorist groups had not disappeared. Believing that another horrific event could happen at any moment, we were propelled by a sense of urgency through many endless hours of work and sleepless nights as we tried to set the FDNY on a stronger foundation. We were concerned about biological and chemical attacks, radiological dirty bombs, and attempts to use improvised explosive devices.

One day, Kate announced that she had put together a Terrorism Preparedness Task Force to advise the FDNY on the types of threats that had historically been beyond our core expertise.

In headquarters, some were wary about Kate's crazy plan, before we learned that she had recruited an impressive international team. It included former CIA Director James Woolsey; former Director-General of Israel's Mossad Shabtai Shavit, to advise on counterterrorism; Commissioner of Israel's Fire and Rescue Authority Shimon Romach; the Nobel laureate in medicine Joshua Lederberg; onetime NYC Health Commissioner and FDA Commissioner Margaret Hamburg, to advise on biological threats; and Greg Canavan, a division head at the Los Alamos National Laboratory, to advise on radiological and nuclear events.

As chief of planning, I found it an enlightening experience to have people of such national and international stature counsel us on the types of threats we now faced and on how we should think about planning for multiple kinds of terrorist attacks. It opened my eyes to a whole new world of terrorism and response to mass casualty incidents.

Dealing with weapons of mass destruction was a reality none of us wanted to hear. But after digesting their high-level input, I realized that it was not a matter of *if* we would be attacked again, but *when*. The critical next step was to imagine some of these ideas in a real-world context and prepare the department to respond.

Enter another 9/11 survivor to develop a preparedness plan for biological terrorism and pandemics: Dr. Kerry Kelly, chief medical doctor for FDNY's Bureau of Health Services.

Dr. Kelly had treated the first firefighter who died on 9/11, Danny Suhr of Engine 216, as well as dozens of other firefighters and civilians. She nearly lost her own life in the collapse. Though she was not a firefighter, Kerry's actions on that day were nothing less than heroic. Her devotion continued with her concern for firefighters' health and the work we would do together for preparedness.

At the time, we were concerned about an aerosolized anthrax attack, a planted smallpox outbreak, and SARS pandemics. We checked on local stockpiles of personal protective equipment (PPE) and appropriate medication.

It was critical to making sure firefighters, police, and health care workers would be in a position to respond to any such event. I traveled to the Centers for Disease Control and Prevention in Atlanta to discuss prioritization for vaccines. CDC staff agreed that first responders would be included with health care workers in the second priority level for vaccinations, medication, and PPE, after the military.

Dr. Kelly, Kate, and I had to figure out a way to distribute medication or a vaccine to on-duty FDNY members without interrupting our response to fires and emergencies.

The result was FDNY's Bio-POD plan, which identified point of distribution (i.e., POD) sites throughout the city that would be staffed by FDNY medical teams. Firefighters and EMS would be called to these locations to receive medication or a vaccine. Starting in 2003, we conducted annual full-scale Bio-POD exercises throughout the city with all on-duty members of the FDNY. To make it more than a simulation, we offered every on-duty member the flu vaccine. This meant we needed a medical staff, vaccine, needles, PPE, computer records, and an incident management team. The FDNY would later use the Bio-POD model during the COVID-19 pandemic to ensure first responders' health, so that they could serve the public.

One of the hardest parts of our job, post-9/11, was to imagine what the future would bring. The FDNY was the world's best at what it has always done: putting out fires. Many in the top ranks thought we should focus on that.

"I promise you that there will be tons of first alarms, second alarms, third alarms, even complicated four- and five-alarm incidents in the next few years," one irate chief said to us at a staff meeting. "But there's only been one 9/11 in all of our history. And you're telling me we're going to change everything because of it?"

There was merit to his viewpoint. Many longed for the days of routine fires and emergencies, using skills, instincts, and knowledge we'd already possessed, rather than accepting the vulnerability of facing something new. But we needed to better understand the threat environment firefighters were now operating in. The Terrorism Preparedness Task Force did that at a strategic level for a few of us. But we had to make that available to firehouses.

From 2001 to 2003, there were multiple anthrax letters, the failed shoe bomber attempt to blow up a plane from Paris to Miami, shootings at LAX Airport in Los Angeles, the Beltway Sniper, a dirty bomb attempt in Chicago, plots to sabotage the Brooklyn Bridge, and dozens of terrorist attacks throughout the world—not to mention NYC's experience with the massive blackout of the Northeast. This weighed on firefighters, and I had to get FDNY's chiefs and company officers to understand the threat environment we faced. They had to comprehend that terrorism was more than what they saw on the news. It is a strategy that uses tactics, like suicide terrorists, to advance a political agenda. For the FDNY to increase preparedness, we had to educate our people about the expanding role of first responders.

Through contacts, Kate found a young U.S. Army major in the social science department at West Point, Reid Sawyer, who was in the early stage of helping to create the Combating Terrorism Center (CTC) at the military academy.

There were striking parallels between the post-9/11 Army and what we were grappling with at the FDNY. There was tension between those who were experts on fighting the last war and the next generation of new leaders who were sure the future would be different. Both organizations craved the skills, expertise, and perspective that understood the threat and challenges ahead.

But things could have easily ground to a halt right there. Not long after Kate started talking to the team at West Point, she was called on the carpet by Scoppetta. Someone thought she was out of line representing the department on her own to the Army and had complained to him.

Frustrated and feeling very misunderstood, Kate came to my office. She and I brainstormed. We needed to give the commissioner more context and decided that bringing me into the West Point relationship would ease some of the concerns. It worked, and on our first trip to West Point, I saw the potential she'd been describing.

We decided to bring the senior leadership from the FDNY to see the possibilities for themselves and cement a relationship with senior leaders at West Point. But asking them to take a day away from the office was a big ask and a gamble.

On a perfect fall day, after being greeted by West Point's superintendent, our group was ushered to the mess hall where all 4,000 cadets eat simultaneously in a matter of minutes, a real logistics phenomenon.

Major Reid Sawyer took us to a balcony called the "Poop Deck" overlooking the mess hall, used to introduce generals and heads of state to the cadets. They called the cadets to attention, and all was quiet. They then introduced the FDNY chief officers from 9/11. In the tradition of West Point, the cadets started to bang their plates in a standing ovation that echoed across the campus and would not stop.

"It's rare for even presidents and generals to get such a reception," Reid said. "The cadets recognize your sacrifices on that day." We were all stunned and moved.

It was a pivotal time for these cadets; they knew that they would be going off to war when they graduated, some to fight al-Qaeda, maybe to hunt down bin Laden. The cadets and firefighters share a common willingness to run into danger. It was an enormous privilege to be honored by them.

After that incredible morning and briefings later that day, we had a mandate to move forward.

It's easy for "partnerships" between institutions to stay high level, to sound great in press releases but not amount to much. We wanted the partnership between West Point's CTC to impact firefighters. Over pizza late one night at Brooklyn headquarters, where Reid, Kate, and I were pushing ourselves to define what that could look like in practice, Reid jumped out of his seat.

"Wait, this is obvious. We're an academic institution that trains leaders to understand threats. Why don't we just train your up-and-coming leaders the same way? And you can train cadets on state and local preparedness and crisis leadership!"

From that conversation, the Counterterrorism Leadership Program was born. This forty-hour executive education program, taught by West Point professors and other experts, combined the latest understanding of the strategic motivation and tactical methods of terrorists.

To teach about leadership and the Middle East, we brought in General John Abizaid, who was in charge of Central Command (the U.S. military commander of the Middle East and later the ambassador to Saudi Arabia). After briefing FDNY senior leadership, we drove the general to the fire academy to teach his class. We heard a second alarm transmitted for a fire in Harlem, not far away.

Immediately, my aide, Ray, asked the general if he wanted to take in the fire. He said yes, and Ray flipped on the red flashing lights. General Abizaid watched the firefighters quickly extinguish the fire, and then he talked to each of them. We got back to the fire academy and told the class that Ray had kidnapped a four-star general.

This course was the first of its kind in the nation designed exclusively for first responders. Over fifteen years, Reid and I taught the Counterterrorism Leadership course to more than 450 FDNY fire and EMS officers, many of whom went on to hold senior leadership positions in the FDNY.

Many of our members said this was the best course they had ever taken. "It changed my life," said one battalion chief. "I was ready to retire, and the course gave me a new purpose to work even harder in the FDNY."

The course dramatically influenced the design of our new $28 million fireboats. By understanding the threat environment, and the possibility of a chlorine attack, we constructed our fireboats to have a pressurized military specs cabin. This meant the fireboat could disperse a drifting vapor cloud with its large-caliber water streams without it killing everyone on board. We also made sure that the water stream of the fireboat could reach the top of the tallest bridge in New York Harbor in case there was a terrorist attack to destroy the bridge with fire. The combination of knowledge and leadership skills was used to protect our Marine Company firefighters and the public.

The CTC invited us to attend an all-day conference for senior leaders, including the FBI. The focus was on understanding the evolving threat environment. Both Major Sawyer and Colonel Russell Howard, founding director of CTC, knew that I needed a security clearance to receive material that would give me, and thus the department, a full and accurate picture. But since I was not law enforcement, there was hesitation. That day, Tim Herlocker, FBI assistant special agent in charge of Intel in the New York Field Office, was present and gave a talk on current threats.

In the Q&A session, Colonel Howard put Agent Herlocker on the spot. "Tim, since FDNY suffered so much on 9/11 and needs to prepare for the next event, would you be willing to sponsor Chief Pfeifer for a security clearance?"

"Ahhh . . . yes, sir," he replied. "I would be proud to start the process for Chief Pfeifer to get a clearance from the FBI."

Tim became a good friend who was able to get me the highest clearances. More importantly, he made sure I got the intelligence the FDNY needed to make critical decisions on preparedness and response.

Once a week, I would go to the JTTF for an interagency intelligence briefing. As soon as I got back to headquarters, I would brief the senior chiefs on any plots against New York City. One particular plot, later reported by the *New York Times*, was against JFK Airport. Since the Fire Department dealt with JFK on a regular basis, I was able to contribute to the building of intelligence. This was a fundamental change. Not only was the FDNY a consumer of intelligence, but we were also a contributor. In other words, we were partners with the intelligence community and law enforcement.

WHILE OUR WORK WITH West Point was fun and inspiring, other tasks, like securing the budget, could not be ignored. In mid-2003, we had to justify to New York City's Office of Management and Budget (OMB) why the FDNY should receive significant federal grant funding for our counterterrorism preparedness efforts. Hayden and I would do the presentation in uniform, but it was up to Kate and me to develop the arguments.

We had to produce an exceptional presentation that could be worth millions of dollars to the FDNY and define how well prepared the city was for the next extreme event. Kate and I knew if we wanted additional funding for our firefighters, we had to touch people's hearts.

Hayden started the presentation by reading a statement that Kate and I had discovered in the Department of Homeland Security documents. Any city that wanted its grant funding must first adopt the National

Incident Management System (NIMS). The Incident Command System was a three-decade-old system that worked at the Pentagon on 9/11 and was now required by the new Department of Homeland Security.

We explained it was critical for agencies to have a unified command system during times of crisis, especially during terrorist attacks. The FDNY had already done this and had trained our people. However, there was resistance from law enforcement, thinking that NIMS was just a fire department system imported from the West Coast.

But we knew that change swiftly happens when funding is the motivating factor. Hayden explained that the NYPD and Office of Emergency Management had to do the same, or the city would forfeit $150 million in grants. That got their attention.

It was now my turn. I knew that most people at OMB took the subway to work.

"It's a little before 9 a.m., and you are getting off the train only minutes from work when you hear a loud boom," I said. "You are okay but shaken by the sound, and then you see a light haze of smoke. This is no ordinary smoke; this is a terrorist chemical attack. You and everyone else are coughing, it is not easy to breathe, and you cannot find your way out. It has only been a few minutes, and things are getting worse, and you cannot even speak to call for help. You think of your family and wonder, who is coming to save you?"

I paused to let that image sink in. There was silence in the room.

"The only agency with self-contained breathing apparatuses for every member and who has some protection from their bunker gear is FDNY. Our firefighters are the ones running in to save you. We need funding to protect them better so they can go home to their families, too."

People were nodding their heads in agreement. It was not that I had scared those decision makers around the table; I gave them hope for surviving the crisis.

Kate gave me a small smile. After her experience on 9/11, the subway scenario deeply resonated with her. The OMB increased FDNY's DHS grants by $20 million annually. They knew that their lives in a chemical attack, and most other kinds of attacks, would depend on firefighters.

A MAGICAL POST-9/11 MOMENT WAS when the FDNY was given a special showing of the movie *The Guys*, starring Sigourney Weaver and Anthony LaPaglia, based on a play by Anne Nelson

The story is about a grief-stricken captain who lost eight men. Anne Nelson, an editor who lived in the neighborhood, stopped by the firehouse to express condolences. Swallowing his pride, the captain asked her for help writing their eulogies. Together, they found the words.

Before showing the film, Anne Nelson and Sigourney Weaver spoke to the audience about the fire company the movie was based on. Kate sat to my left.

"I know that captain and the fire company," I told Kate. "It's about the captain of Ladder 15, which is part of Battalion 1. These were my guys."

Ladder 15, with Lieutenant Joe Leavey and his firefighters, had been in the South Tower with Battalion Chief Orio Palmer. On radio transmissions, we had heard Leavey talking to his guys as they rescued people shortly before the collapse of the South Tower.

Now the captain of Ladder 15 had to talk about "the guys" at each of their funerals. The captain resembled Mr. Rogers, a mild-mannered person who saw the best in everyone. I enjoyed going down to his firehouse near the South Street Seaport. It was not easy for him or any captain to find the right words to describe the unique traits and personalities of the ordinary heroes who were part of his firehouse family.

About halfway through, the movie flashed to real footage of a firefighter's 9/11 funeral.

My heart skipped a beat as I recognized the scene outside the church. The line of firefighters at attention in dress blue uniforms stretched for blocks. Slowly the casket of the hero firefighter resting on top of a fire engine passed.

Shocked, I turned to Kate and whispered, "Oh my God, that is my brother's funeral." She gently touched my hand. As a chief at a public event, I had to keep up my stoic appearance. But it was not easy.

AFTER BEING TOUCHED BY THE MOVIE, I saw the play version of *The Guys* with Ginny at the Museum of Jewish Heritage in Battery Park City, only a few blocks from WTC. The context was powerful. Being at the Holocaust museum pointed to other crimes against humanity, each with deeply personal stories of human suffering and emerging from the unthinkable.

Walking through the Holocaust museum reminded me of the words of Anne Frank, writing in 1944: "It's difficult in times like these: ideals, dreams, and cherished hopes rise within us, only to be crushed by grim reality. It's a wonder I haven't abandoned all my ideals; they seem so absurd and impractical. Yet, I cling to them because I still believe, in spite of everything, that people are truly good at heart."

In the aftermath of 9/11, there was so much pain and, for many, anger. While that anger was properly directed at terrorist groups like al-Qaeda, some were wrongly blaming an entire religion. I believed, like

Anne Frank, that people were "truly good at heart" as we came together to help each other after this tragedy.

One afternoon, I was at the FBI field office down the block from the Duane Street firehouse for an Intel briefing by Assistant Special Agent in Charge Tim Herlocker on the most current terrorist threats. After the meeting, he asked if I was interested in going with him to a Ramadan service at a mosque, followed by a light dinner. The FBI was trying to build bridges with the Muslim community, since there had been a lot of anti-Islam sentiment in the aftermath of the attacks.

I immediately said yes. I saw this as an opportunity to make a difference by reaching out to the Muslim community. In my white shirt with the FDNY logo, I took my shoes off and sat on the floor for evening prayer, amid dozens of men from the community and my two FBI friends.

The imam announced that the fast was broken. Then we ate dates, prayed, and broke bread together. The president of the mosque was glad to see me and said, with a heavy heart, "We saw firefighters from the local firehouses on Staten Island leave for the World Trade Center, and we saw that many of them never came back, which broke our hearts." He wanted me to know that his community grieved the loss of their neighborhood firefighters.

In my own way, I was saying that we are in this together and trust in each other's goodness.

20

GLOWING RED

In April 2004, at a small restaurant in Monterey, California, a fire chief, police chief, CIA agent, and FBI special agent were having dinner together. We were classmates in a master's degree program at the Center for Homeland Defense and Security at the Naval Postgraduate School.

Our discussion turned to our testimony at the ongoing hearings being held by the 9/11 Commission. The FBI agent from Minneapolis described his experience when he wanted to obtain a search warrant to search Zacarias Moussaoui's computer hard drive. Moussaoui would later become known as the twentieth hijacker, tasked to fly a plane into the White House or Capitol but instead was arrested in August 2001.

The special agent had become so frustrated with a system that lacked any urgency for gathering and sharing information that, at one point, he blurted out to supervisors that he was "just trying to stop someone from taking a plane and crashing it into the World Trade Center." His statement—like Fire Marshal Ronnie Bucca's warning—turned out to be prophetic.

Then I talked about my experience as the first fire chief at the World Trade Center. I related how I'd heard stories that NYPD helicopters circling the buildings from above had transmitted urgent messages to their officers to get out—information that had not been shared with the FDNY. For twenty-nine minutes on 9/11, I had not known a whole building had collapsed. Though I had immediately given an evacuation order, how many firefighters could have been saved if I had known the North Tower was likely to collapse?

Our firsthand accounts illustrated how the CIA and FBI, as well as the FDNY and NYPD, did not share information at critical times. I knew in my heart that it was not intentional by anyone to withhold vital information. But why, when it counted the most, was information not shared?

The 9/11 Commission had started holding hearings into the circumstances surrounding the attacks. After taking testimony from those in the intelligence and law enforcement communities, the commission had reported that the system was "blinking red" with many warnings in the months before the attack.

In January 2004, Pete Hayden and I were asked to testify. I was happy to tell the story, but I had a bigger goal in mind: to get agencies to work together.

In front of a handful of the commission's staffers, in a big conference room at FDNY headquarters, we described the events of that day, backed up by video from the Naudets' film. The staggering loss of life remained as horrific as it had been almost three years earlier. Even though one of the FDNY lawyers had heard much of the story before, she was in tears.

Repeatedly during the six-hour proceedings, I asked the commission to include one sentence in their report: "On 9/11, first responders at the World Trade Center attacks had stovepipe situational awareness." The intent was to mirror the commission's earlier reporting of a lack of intelligence sharing between the FBI and CIA, which they called "stovepiped." Information, like smoke, flowed only one way: up the stovepipe flue.

Everyone who responded that day was doing the best they could to save lives under extreme conditions. But there were issues we had to make public, key among them the habit of using separate command posts and the failure to share information.

I had to dispel the misconception that this was purely a technology issue with radios. The real 9/11 disconnect was a behavioral problem. At the time, I had little knowledge about political forces that push back on things that are difficult to hear. I was merely trying to get first responders to share information so we could handle the next large-scale disasters. But I did not succeed. Even though I called the commission back so I could testify for an additional four hours, stressing the importance of situational awareness, my phrase "stovepipe situational awareness" was not included. However, they did include my point on the importance of information sharing between agencies.

Two years later, when one of the 9/11 commissioners spoke at the Harvard Kennedy School, I learned that they thought it was too painful for the American people to hear that New York City's esteemed first responders did not talk to each other.

FOR YEARS, I wondered what the NYPD's helicopter pilots had said to each other and to their dispatchers, and what they'd broadcast over the radio to members of the police force at the WTC. We needed that material during our work on the McKinsey Report. But the radio transmissions were considered so sensitive that the NYPD steadfastly declined to make them public.

After years of searching, I got the NYPD helicopter radio transmissions from two sources: the 9/11 Commission and investigative reporters Jim Dwyer and Kevin Flynn from the *New York Times*. These transmissions revealed that the NYPD had had much more knowledge of what was happening than did the FDNY.

At 9:59 a.m., when the South Tower collapsed, an NYPD helicopter pilot immediately radioed that it had fallen and advised everyone in the complex to evacuate the other buildings.

An Emergency Service Unit police officer in the North Tower heard the message but couldn't comprehend how a 110-story building could collapse, so he asked that the message be repeated. The next transmission reiterated that the South Tower was gone and that the North Tower was in imminent danger of coming down as well.

At 10:07 a.m., the pilot of Aviation 14 advised that the top fifteen stories of the North Tower looked like they were "glowing red. It's inevitable." Only a minute later, the pilot of Aviation 6 reported: "I don't think this has too much longer to go. I would evacuate all people within the area of the second building."

At 10:20 a.m.: "NYPD Aviation Unit reports that the top of the tower might be leaning."

That was followed a minute later with this: "NYPD Aviation Unit reports that the North Tower is buckling on the southeast corner and leaning to the south . . . NYPD officer advises that all personnel close to the building pull back three blocks in every direction."

And finally, at 10:27 a.m.: "NYPD Aviation Unit reports that the roof is going to come down very shortly."

Each subsequent message had a cumulative effect of added urgency, plus multiple validations of the original report. Eyewitnesses indicated that ESU officers evacuated so quickly that, at one point, they were sliding down stair banisters.

The situation for the FDNY was vastly different. At 9:59 a.m., firefighters in the North Tower heard a violent roar but did not know what had happened. Most firefighters in the North Tower had no idea how dire the situation was during the following twenty-nine minutes, nor did I. What the world saw on the news, we could not see.

The lack of available information for the Fire Department translated into an unhurried evacuation—with lethal consequences. I radioed to firefighters, "Evacuate the building!" Had I known the full picture, my message to evacuate would have been preceded with the words, "Mayday, mayday, mayday"—signaling the urgency to get out of the building. I could only imagine how that warning would have been a game changer for all of us in the North Tower, including my brother and Engine 33.

It was painful to ponder the idea that many deaths could have been avoided had the FDNY and NYPD shared situational awareness. Some observers wanted to reduce this issue to only a technological problem with the repeater radio.

An investigation by the National Institute of Standards and Technology (NIST) found that the WTC repeater was incapable of working in the critical moments after the South Tower had collapsed and would not have assisted in the evacuation of firefighters from the North Tower. The debris from the South Tower destroyed the repeater located in WTC-5 that received a command channel message on one frequency and rebroadcast the signal on another frequency at a higher wattage.

It turned out that we were lucky that the chiefs in the North Tower were not on the WTC repeater channel. If those of us in the North Tower had been using the repeater, all communication would have ended. Even if you were standing next to each other, you would not have heard any radio transmission. Like a mobile phone, without the cellular tower, you have no communications.

Since then, I made sure that every FDNY response vehicle with a radio has the handie-talkie radio frequencies programmed into the vehicle's high-powered 25-watt radios. With an innovation from Captain Mike Stein, we also created a portable high-powered post radio, the size of an attaché case, to carry inside a building. This avoids having a single point of communications failure.

However, even with the best technology in the world, if agencies don't talk to each other, there is no communication. The 9/11 Commission reported that the radios were "not the primary cause of firefighter fatalities in the North Tower" and confirmed that my evacuation messages were indeed heard. NIST also concluded that emergency responders' lives were likely lost resulting from the lack of timely information sharing.

However, these reports did not answer the most important question: *Why* did the NYPD and FDNY not talk to each other? What could have caused this behavior during extreme events? Why wasn't a unified command set up at the WTC, the way Chief Jim Schwartz of the Arlington County Fire Department and FBI Special Agent Christopher Combs did at the Pentagon that same day? Regardless of any prior power struggles among first responders in NYC, it is inconceivable that anyone on 9/11 would ever consciously withhold vital information that could potentially save lives. I had to find out *why*—for my guys and all first responders.

. . .

THE INCIDENT COMMAND POST WAS established on 9/11 by FDNY opposite both burning towers on the far side of West Street. Yet, even with fire and smoke coming from the top of the WTC, the NYPD set up a separate command post on Church Street, on the opposite side of the WTC, more than a block and a half away.

This was the primary fatal flaw. By not colocating command posts, agencies became hyperfocused on their own tasks.

Such behavior is strengthened by agencies implicitly thinking of themselves as being the most important. Police and fire department cultures reinforce a sense of belonging to an exceptional group. These organizations call themselves the "Finest" (NYPD) and "Bravest" (FDNY).

As the intensity of the WTC crisis mounted, police commanders failed to recognize that the reports from helicopters would be of crucial importance to the Fire Department.

Not only did the NYPD fail to tell us, the FDNY never asked!

Turning toward one's own group during a crisis is an inevitable part of the stress response. The brain produces a neurological cocktail of stress hormones, which helps first responders like cops and firefighters do their jobs at critical points in a crisis.

Adrenaline and cortisol help our minds become more alert and focused and our muscles more energy efficient. These hormones are credited for producing the fight-or-flight response. Police officers who heard transmissions from helicopters that the building might collapse had a stress response of *flight* and quickly evacuated the North Tower.

Dopamine assists us in decision making by allowing us to match past experiences and learned knowledge to the present incident. Firefighters quickly scan their memories to see if the present situation relates to the past, thus giving us a clue of what to do, like knowing how to search for trapped people.

The pilots who saw the South Tower collapse quickly concluded that the same failure could happen to the North Tower. This pattern match led to being hyperfocused on radioing police dispatchers and ESU police officers on the alarming conditions.

In her book *The Upside of Stress*, psychologist Kelly McGonigal tells us that the stress response also stimulates the pituitary gland to produce the neurohormone oxytocin.

"When oxytocin is released as part of the stress response, it's encouraging you to connect with your support network," McGonigal says. Under stress, firefighters want to be near other firefighters, and cops want to be near other cops.

Thus, oxytocin reinforces organizational bias; you turn to your own group so you don't feel alone and to protect people you care about. It made perfect sense for police pilots and commanders to call for an evacuation to protect their members from imminent collapse.

As the incident's stress and complexity increased, it became more difficult for commanders to focus on anything outside their operational world. If only NYPD incident commanders had been standing next to FDNY incident commanders, the stress response would have strengthened the bond between commanders, and there would have been a sense of joint responsibility for all first responders. Instead, the NYPD focused on the urgent evacuation of its own members, thinking someone else would tell the FDNY.

An NYPD friend whose children were on a swim team with my kids told me he knew one of the helicopter pilots. I asked him if he could arrange for me to speak with the pilot.

It was an informal call, and he was happy to talk to me. He explained that about five minutes after the collapse of the South Tower, he observed the North Tower from the air and transmitted to NYPD Central Dispatch that it was also in danger of collapse, that "the top fifteen floors are glowing red." He speculated that it wouldn't be much longer before the building fell.

"I assumed it was going to be relayed to the Fire Department," he told me. "I never thought about calling you guys." He thought somebody else would warn us, either police dispatch or police command. But that never happened.

At last, I had figured out that people naturally turn to their own groups under stress, which was the reason why agencies did not talk to each other. But fixing the social force of organizational bias—seemingly hardwired by our stress responses—wouldn't be so easy.

FOR A WHILE, my aide Ray and I pursued the idea of getting the FDNY helicopters. We'd have our own view of an incident that was not dependent on the NYPD. A cool concept, but financially and politically unfeasible.

"Why not get news video streams from news helicopters?" Ray suggested. He set up meetings for me with major network TV news stations to discuss a collaborative agreement to supply the FDNY with live video feed directly to our new, high-tech Fire Department Operations Center.

In return for video, we would explain to the reporters what they were seeing. WPIX and ABC were the first to sign a memorandum of collaboration, followed by the other networks. This was a unique and valued public-private partnership.

Once we had the news helicopters, we wanted to get the video feeds from police helicopters for major fires or unusual events because they can go into restricted airspace.

I set up a meeting at JFK Airport between me, the chief of NYPD Aviation, air traffic controllers, and the Federal Aviation Administration (FAA). I had to tread carefully not to alienate anyone.

I explained how we were getting video from news helicopters and asked the NYPD for the same. To my surprise, they agreed without putting up a fight. I wasn't sure if the jets taking off in the background reminded them of 9/11, but I was delighted and thanked them.

However, I also wanted a fire chief in the police helicopter to have, as Ray put it, "eyes in the sky." The chief of Aviation was blunt. "No, this is a police helicopter and not the place for a fire chief."

Ray had done his homework. FAA rules state, "A helicopter can be used as a tool for the fire department during a fire or emergency." This meant that a helicopter under the control of the FDNY could operate in restricted airspace during an emergency.

Armed with Ray's research, I turned to the FAA representative.

"If I place a fire chief in a news helicopter and make this a tool of FDNY, will the helicopter be allowed to enter the twenty-five-mile restricted airspace in an emergency that only the police helicopter can operate in?"

"In the case you described," the senior official said, "the helicopter is a tool of the FDNY and would be allowed in the restricted airspace."

I knew the NYPD did not want news helicopters flying into what they considered "their airspace." Maybe the prospect of sharing airspace with us would prompt them to share their helicopters instead.

The chief of NYPD Aviation stared at me in disbelief, then agreed that a fire chief would be allowed in an NYPD helicopter at major fires and emergencies. Having multiple eyes in the sky would provide greater situational awareness to both agencies. He just needed to take the facts to his bosses. We negotiated an agreement for video and stipulated that a battalion chief would be assigned to the NYPD helicopter at every third-alarm fire or unusual incident, which became a joint operating procedure.

Another of Ray's ideas that I pushed forward was creating the Command Tactical Unit. He and Ralph Bernard, head of the department's Audio Visual Unit, used firefighters responding with an old ambulance to take video footage from the rear of burning buildings—areas that a chief cannot see from the street. Later, the FDNY acquired drones that now provide images from above.

Change was taking place between the FDNY and NYPD. We had to connect, collaborate, and coordinate with each other before thinking about command and control of an incident. In September 2004, right after the 9/11 Commission Report was released, I created FDNY's Center for Terrorism and Disaster Preparedness (CTDP), which focused on bringing diverse agencies together to prepare for extreme events. We shared intelligence reports, developed emergency response plans, and exercised response procedures to terrorism and disasters.

BUILDING THIS NETWORK OF PARTNERS took months. We followed an old French recipe from Jules's grandmother for building trust: "Start with cooking and sharing a meal together."

Before planning meetings at the CTDP, members of the agencies would first sit down and have a hearty firehouse-cooked lunch. Now as FDNY's first Chief of Counterterrorism and Emergency Preparedness, I developed close partnerships with OEM, NYPD's Counterterrorism Bureau and Special Operations Bureau, including ESU. But would this French recipe make a difference at the next big event?

On January 15, 2009, we got a chance to find out. In the famous "Miracle on the Hudson," Captain Chesley "Sully" Sullenberger and co-pilot Jeff Skiles crash-landed their disabled Airbus A320, carrying 155 passengers and crew, into the icy cold waters of the Hudson River just south of the George Washington Bridge connecting New York and New Jersey. With the US Airways plane floating downriver, passengers scrambled onto its wings and into lifeboats.

Almost immediately, we received the "crash box" from LaGuardia Airport and multiple 911 calls reporting a plane crash in the Hudson River.

Instead of racing to the scene, I remained at headquarters to command the FDOC. Sal Cassano, now chief of department, arrived and wanted a briefing before running off to the scene. We didn't know geese had caused the crash; we were still trying to rule out a terrorist attack. I grabbed Cassano by the arm. "Sal, you need to stay here in case there are other planes." Reluctantly, he remained at the FDOC.

Within minutes of people standing on the wings of the plane, a NY Waterway ferry pulled up alongside the floating aircraft and took off fifty-six people. FDNY's Marine Unit 1A rescued twenty passengers. Two small boats from the U.S. Coast Guard and six other NY Waterway ferries removed the rest. Meanwhile, NYPD divers and FDNY's Cold Water Rescue Unit searched the sinking plane to make sure no one had been left behind.

As the various boats arrived at piers in New York and New Jersey, forty-five passengers and five crew members were taken to ten different hospitals, while 105 shivering passengers in wet clothes were treated for hypothermia with blankets at the scene by EMS and the Red Cross. Our

EMS personnel recorded all these patient contacts. The urgent question was how to know if everyone was accounted for, including two nonticketed small children.

While all this was occurring, agency incident commanders set up a unified command post at Pier 81. As the plane drifted down the river at about five knots per hour, a second CP was established at Chelsea Piers. Incident commanders were chasing the damaged plane down the river.

Inside the FDOC, we received live-feed video images from police and news helicopters. The FDNY provided information to first responders, hospitals, law enforcement, and emergency operations centers. Overall, we had more situational awareness than the chiefs at the scene, so we transmitted what we knew to them as soon as possible.

But the greatest value of being at the FDOC was to collect information about who was on the plane. In a small conference room, we compared on two large-screen smart TVs the manifest from LaGuardia Airport of passengers and crew on the plane with the list from our EMS of people who came off the plane.

Within fifteen minutes, the EMS officers emerged and told Chief Cassano and me that everyone on board was accounted for.

"Go back and check the data one more time," I said. When they returned, their ranking officer told me, "Chief, all 155 passengers and crew are alive and rescued." Cassano immediately notified the fire commissioner, who informed the mayor.

I had one of my lieutenants sign into the Homeland Security Information Network (HSIN), a federal government platform for information sharing with local, state, tribal, and territorial authorities: "FDNY confirms that all 155 passengers and crew of US Airways Flight 1549 are alive and rescued."

Within a minute, I got a call from the Department of Homeland

Security's undersecretary of Intelligence and Analysis, Charles Allen, asking if the information was accurate. I said, "Yes, sir, it is correct." He called the DHS secretary, Michael Chertoff, who then called the White House Situation Room. It was amazing to think there were only two or three degrees of separation between the president of the United States and me.

Late that afternoon, Mayor Bloomberg held a press briefing describing the passengers' ordeal and praising the crew and first responders, including the private ferries, for their fast and brave rescue of passengers. He also said the unified command had contributed to saving everyone.

Interoperability for voice, video, and data was critical for connecting first responders. However, as Cassano said, "If radios are interoperable, but you don't talk to each other, you might as well throw the radios in the water."

Having the technology is only part of the equation. The Miracle on the Hudson was a success story for interagency cooperation in rescuing everyone aboard US Airways Flight 1549. And it highlighted the quick thinking and bravery of two ordinary heroes, Sullenberger and Skiles.

UNDERSTANDING WHY FIRST RESPONDERS ACT the way they do enabled us to overcome organizational bias that hampered response on 9/11. Police, fire, and other agencies were working together and trusting each other. But just around the corner, we would face new challenges.

On May 10, 2010, Faisal Shahzad, a homegrown terrorist, drove his car into Manhattan and stopped it at the center of the intersection of 45th Street and 7th Avenue. He hoped to explode a powerful car bomb as a terrorist act in the middle of Times Square. After he attempted to ignite the charge to set off the bomb, something went wrong and smoke started to emanate from the car. An alert pedestrian pointed the car out to a mounted police officer. Initially, the police officer, thinking this was routine, notified the Fire Department of a car fire. Engine Company 54 and Ladder Company 4 responded.

The SUV was still running, but the owner was nowhere to be found. White smoke poured from the vehicle, rather than the usual black smoke found in car fires. An FDNY handheld thermal-imaging camera showed that the engine and brakes, as would be expected, were hot. The rest of the car exhibited no sign of heat or fire, just an odor of fireworks emanating from the rear of the vehicle. One fire lieutenant realized that "something did not look right." Instead of continuing with routine operations, the fire officers asked a police officer to run the license plate. When the police officer came back and reported the plate was not registered to that vehicle, both fire and police officers—now aware of possible terrorist scenarios—suspected an improvised explosive device and immediately evacuated the area, potentially saving hundreds of people.

I was both relieved that we had averted a tragedy and excited that the FDNY and NYPD were sharing information and beginning to work together. With the success of our French recipe and experiences, we created a city protocol that requires incident commanders to be within "arm's distance" of each other at a unified command post. Yet I couldn't help but wonder what the next extreme event would be.

21

———

SMOLDERING EMBERS

AFTER EXTINGUISHING ANY BLAZE, firefighters search for remaining pockets of hidden flames so they can put them out. Otherwise, the embers will grow into another inferno. The situation on 9/11 was no different. The deadly smoldering embers of 9/11 continued to burn long after the event.

I could not bear to think of history repeating itself. I owed it to my firefighters to understand how these buildings, made of thick steel and concrete, had crumpled so fast and so completely. What would fire chiefs need to know to make decisions about sending firefighters into skyscrapers that come under attack?

Many people assumed that the impact of the planes caused the buildings to fall. In fact, it was the fires that brought down the World Trade Center. Fire, one of the world's most ancient weapons, was used against our modern metropolis.

Leslie Robertson, the chief WTC engineer at the time of its construction, told journalists that he had considered the possibility of a Boeing 707, among the largest commercial aircraft at the time, hitting the building.

However, he did not design for thousands of gallons of fuel being released into the building and the potential damage fire would cause. Such omission was another example of a failure of imagination.

The National Institute of Standards and Technology began its engineering investigation into the unprecedented collapses of the three WTC buildings around the same time as the 9/11 Commission.

I had many discussions with Dr. Shyam Sunder, the lead investigator for NIST, during the examination of the collapse of the Twin Towers. "The Towers withstood the impact," he said, "and would have remained standing were it not for the dislodged insulation [fireproofing] and the subsequent multiple-floor fires." Much of the jet fuel burned off on impact but ignited fires on multiple floors. The high-temperature fires weakened the columns that were not severed to the point of buckling, causing a progressive collapse.

In 2008, NIST finished its investigation of WTC-7, the forty-seven-story office building whose occupants had included the CIA, the Secret Service, and New York City's Office of Emergency Management. I invited Dr. Sunder to brief me, Fire Commissioner Scoppetta, and Chief of Department Cassano on why WTC-7, which was not hit by a plane, collapsed at 5:20 p.m. that evening.

He explained that, when the North Tower collapsed, the debris started fires on multiple floors in WTC-7. Fueled by ordinary office furnishings, the fire quickly spread to numerous floors. As windows broke from the heat, fresh air rushed in and intensified the flames. Without water for the sprinkler system, we decided not to send firefighters into the building, and the fire raged out of control. Those elements, combined with fire-induced thermal expansion of steel girders and the particular building design, created a "perfect storm" that triggered the collapse.

Sunder dispelled conspiracy theories that had started to flourish by definitively stating that fire caused the collapse. This would make Osama bin Laden the world's most wanted arsonist.

I feared that terrorists could cause another 9/11 without the planes. We could not afford any more failures of imagination. I had to warn about extremists using fire as a weapon in future attacks on high-rise buildings. I published articles that appeared in fire journals cautioning chiefs not to risk firefighters if a high-rise building might collapse. Later I met with government agencies and the Secretary of Homeland Security, testified before Congress, and spoke at the United Nations warning that extremists would again use fire as a weapon in the form of "vertical terrorism" against towering skyscrapers.

FOR almost a decade, I had wondered if Osama bin Laden, the leader of al-Qaeda responsible for the 9/11 attacks and so many other terrorist acts, would be caught. Late on the evening of May 2, 2011, I no longer needed to wonder as the world was told of the previous day's raid.

President Barack Obama, standing in the East Room of the White House, announced: "The United States has conducted an operation that killed Osama bin Laden, the leader of al-Qaeda, and a terrorist who's responsible for the murder of thousands of innocent men, women, and children.

"It was nearly ten years ago that a bright September day was darkened by the worst attack on the American people in our history. The images of 9/11 are seared into our national memory—hijacked planes cutting through a cloudless September sky; the Twin Towers collapsing to the ground; black smoke billowing up from the Pentagon; the wreckage of Flight 93 in Shanksville, Pennsylvania, where the actions of heroic citizens saved even more heartbreak and destruction.

"And yet we know that the worst images are those that were unseen to the world. The empty seat at the dinner table. Children who were forced to grow up without their mother or their father. Parents who would never know the feeling of their child's embrace. Nearly 3,000 citizens taken from us, leaving a gaping hole in our hearts."

A sense of relief came over me as another 9/11 chapter ended. On TV, firefighters could be seen cheering atop their fire trucks in Times Square. On the side of one truck, you could see the names of fifteen members lost from one firehouse. Finally, this open wound could be closed.

A month after the U.S. military brought bin Laden to justice, I and Sal Cassano, now fire commissioner, heard the details directly from the CIA. Brian Gimlett, a retired Secret Service agent in charge, invited Cassano and me to come to the New York Stock Exchange, where Brian was senior vice president of global security.

As we sat in a secure room, Brian introduced two women from the CIA, Gina Haspel, who would later become the director of the Agency, and an analyst in her twenties who had played a significant role in finding bin Laden.

The CIA analyst spoke to us for thirty minutes. It was the best, most intense briefing I ever received in my career. From her passion and conviction, I knew that she had pushed hard in her quest to find bin Laden.

She and fellow agents pieced small bits of information together to track one particular courier to a compound in Abbottabad, Pakistan. Though many in the CIA believed bin Laden had to be in Afghanistan, she thought this courier would lead the Agency and Special Forces to bin Laden. She had met with President Obama, Director of the CIA Leon

Panetta, and other government officials to outline what she had discovered, trying to persuade the president to approve a dangerous mission.

Senior officials thought that the chances of bin Laden being at the Abbottabad compound were at best 60 percent. When it came time for this young analyst to speak, she insisted that the odds were 90 percent. In reality, the analyst told me, she believed the odds were closer to 100 percent, but it would "freak everyone out" if she said that. The meeting led to Operation Neptune Spear, overseen by Admiral William McRaven and successfully conducted by Navy SEAL Team Six in Abbottabad.

At the end of the meeting, the analyst came up to me and said, "Chief, I have something for you."

Since the attacks, each time the United States captured or killed a 9/11 terrorist, President Bush had put an X through the name on a list of key al-Qaeda operatives even after he was out of office. The CIA had continued that practice. After this most recent operation, President Bush had X-ed out the name of Osama bin Laden.

It gave me a brief flashback to September 14, 2001, at Ground Zero, when President Bush had quietly told us, "We will get them." The seamless dedication of the CIA and Special Forces across two administrations made this possible.

She stretched out her right hand with a coin bearing an X nestled in her palm. As we shook hands, she passed me the coin. In return, I presented her with my coin, symbolizing the FDNY Center for Terrorism and Disaster Preparedness.

A couple of weeks later, we had lunch together. She showed me a picture on her phone of a red and blue standing cardboard poster that was part of the 9/11 exhibition at CIA headquarters in Langley, Virginia. One side read: "He survived." The other side read: "She remembers." She told me the poster represented the two of us. I was the person she'd remembered from the 9/11 film. About a year after our lunch, I would remember her when she was portrayed as Maya in the film *Zero Dark Thirty*.

Osama bin Laden had been brought to justice, but the casualties from the attacks would continue.

IN THE YEARS SINCE 9/11, we had become aware of the devastating health impact of the toxic dust and smoke that permeated lower Manhattan after the collapses. Finding more and more of our members were coming down with respiratory illness and cancers, the FDNY had instituted a yearly medical evaluation for its 9/11 responders.

In 2008, Ray Pfeifer was diagnosed with cancer related to his work on the Pile. Ray could have retired after recovering from major surgery, but instead, he returned to light duty. He drove me for a while. But cancer took its toll, slowing Ray down.

A couple of years after Ray's diagnosis, 9/11-induced disease hit the Duane Street firehouse. Firefighter John O'Neill, the chauffeur, and Lieutenant Randy Wiebicke of Ladder 1, who'd toiled tirelessly on the Pile, both died of cancer. So did retired Chief Larry Byrnes, who'd come back to help that day and for weeks following. Though most of their Engine 7, Ladder 1, and Battalion 1 colleagues had moved on to other firehouses or other jobs, we returned for their line-of-duty funerals. Over the last twenty years, more than 240 FDNY members have died from 9/11-related diseases. By the time of the twenty-fifth anniversary, we fear that more firefighters will have died from inhaling 9/11 dust than the 343 who died that day.

Ray continued to work at our Center for Terrorism and Disaster Preparedness between periods of medical leave and light duty. He would tell me his ideas for the center and give me good-natured kidding. When I got promoted to assistant chief, Ray hung a sign from the auditorium balcony reading, "Congratulations, Joey Three-Star."

After his retirement, Ray concentrated on a new passion: lobbying Congress to extend and expand the James Zadroga 9/11 Health and Compensation Act (2011), named after an NYPD police officer whose death was linked to exposure to toxic dust and fumes. The bill provided medical monitoring and care to sick first responders, workers, survivors, and others contaminated by the dust.

On trips to the Capitol in Washington, D.C., Ray, accompanied by comedian Jon Stewart, waited in the hallways of Congress for lawmakers to pass by so they could ask for their vote on the bill. No matter how long it took, Ray sat patiently in his wheelchair as Stewart paced back and forth. Securing votes one by one was exhausting for Ray, but he never let on that he was in pain. He only said, "It's all good."

Stewart described how legislators and their staffers would hand Ray their business cards to brush him off. Ray would point to his pocket and say, "I have all the cards I need." He had the memorial cards of the members of his firehouse and other units who had died on 9/11. These were two-by-four-inch cards with the person's picture, along with personal details on the back.

It would infuriate Stewart to see such disrespect for Ray in uniform. But eventually, Ray won lawmakers over and secured enough votes to pass the reauthorization of the bill in 2015. For Ray's selfless work on the Pile and his concern for first responders, he received the Key to the City of New York from Mayor Bill de Blasio in 2016. Of course, Ray was grateful, but he didn't need keys to open doors; he used his heart.

Less than a year and a half later, I got a call from Ray's brother. He said, "You need to come to see Ray right away." I rushed to the hospice.

During Ray's battle with 9/11 cancer, I would ask him how he was doing, and Ray would always say, "All good." But this time was different. Ray was so critically sick that he could not speak, yet he was awake. In the quiet hospice room, I told him what a great friend he was and kissed him on his forehead. As I stepped back, I could feel emotions welling up inside of me. And in the silence, Ray said with his eyes, "All good." When I left the room, that was the last time I saw my friend Ray.

22

———

THE WHOLE WORLD
ON FIRE

IN THE FALL OF 2012, a North Atlantic hurricane merged with a nor'easter to create "Superstorm Sandy." As it slammed into New York City on October 29, at the peak of high tide during a full moon, Sandy brought a storm surge of 13.8 feet and 65-mile-per-hour sustained winds, with gusts up to 92 miles per hour. The storm, almost a thousand miles in diameter, became the most significant and damaging Atlantic Basin hurricane to hit the East Coast of the United States in centuries.

I was monitoring weather conditions when I learned that a spark had ignited an inferno in Breezy Point, our childhood summer place where I had joined the Rockaway Point Volunteer Fire Department and learned to love firefighting.

Breezy Point held more recent precious memories for me, too. Kevin and I had sailed the waters of Jamaica Bay and the Atlantic Ocean surrounding Breezy Point. When our kids were small, Ginny and I would stay with the kids, my parents, and my brother in the bungalow. Kevin and I took Christine and Greg on their first sailboat ride and taught them how to sail. Kevin's old Hobie Cat was stored under the cottage.

When my parents had gotten too elderly to maintain the bungalow, Greg bought it and turned it into a beautiful year-round home. Each summer, he had my parents stay with him, which brought back healing memories of good times with Kevin.

On the Breezy Point bayside, a piece of WTC steel stands at a 9/11 memorial for this community, where so many members of the FDNY and NYPD live. The steel overlooks the place where we kept my brother's catamaran during the summer, and across the bay in the background is the New York City skyline with the new World Trade Center.

Despite everything that had happened on 9/11 and all the losses, I had come to love the job again.

Now, high winds, coupled with the storm surge, had created a short in a transformer, which ignited the electrical box in a single-story home just off the ocean. The house was owned by the parents of my childhood friend Brian Jordan, who'd grown up to become a Franciscan priest. During 9/11 recovery operations, Father Jordan had said mass every week under a tall piece of steel in the shape of a cross at Ground Zero. Luckily, neither he nor his family were in the house when the fire erupted.

Hurricane-force winds whipped the flames from house to house. Directly in the path of this wind-driven fire was my son Gregory's house. Before I arrived, the fire was only eight houses away.

At 10 p.m., after hearing reports of flooding and multiple fires along the narrow Rockaway peninsula, I responded to Breezy Point while other staff chiefs were deployed throughout the city.

Driving myself, I had to zigzag through Brooklyn and Queens to avoid flooded roads. Crossing the Marine Parkway Bridge over the crashing waves of Jamaica Bay, I saw Breezy Point shrouded in complete darkness, except for an enormous fiery glow reflecting off clouds. The two-mile road leading to Breezy Point appeared to be a fierce river, completely covered by three feet of roiling water. Unable to proceed any farther in my SUV, I pulled over on dry land and got into my bunker gear. Standing at the mouth of this raging river, I flagged down the next responding fire rig.

Engine 10, from Ten House opposite the WTC, stopped to pick me up.

The coincidence was surreal. Eleven years earlier, I had been the first chief to arrive at the WTC attacks, along with firefighters from Ten House. And now, here we were, the first units to respond to another major disaster that was growing more dangerous by the moment.

The engine smoked and the exhaust gurgled like a boat while the chauffeur plowed through two miles of streets flooded as high as the apparatus's headlights.

From the crew seats in the back of Engine 10, I directed the captain to make sure the Engine company chauffeur did not take his foot off the gas. If he did, the engine would stall out, and we would have to swim. During this short but treacherous ride, I thought about how I started as a volunteer firefighter in Rockaway Point, how that led me to the FDNY, and all that followed. I also thought about seeing the faces of Engine 10 in the lobby of the North Tower before I ordered them to go up to help those in need. Some, like Lieutenant Gregg Atlas, never made it back to Ten House.

As we pulled into Breezy Point, all I could see was that eerie orange cloud growing larger across the night sky. I instructed the chauffeur to take a hydrant at the northern edge of the fire, which was on a new water main. I was battered by wind, rain, and smoke as I waded through water a foot deep.

By midnight, we had more than a hundred houses ablaze, forcing firefighters to battle this growing inferno on multiple fronts. The firestorm showered the area with burning embers the size of golf balls. I tried to duck, but one of those blazing embers caught me on the left side of my face. Adrenaline pumping, I didn't even feel it, but I knew I was burned. That was the least of my worries. I was concerned about my firefighters' safety. There were hidden dangers everywhere. In some spots, water was five feet deep. The saturated ground was like quicksand; you could sink down to your hips. And the fire was as hot as hell.

The rapidly moving fire drove flames to the west and north, consuming building after building, block after block. The conflagration became its own perfect storm, combining ample combustible material—the wooden bungalows—hurricane-force winds, little water pressure in the hydrants, difficult access, and few firefighting resources.

Without a reliable water source, battling intense, wind-driven flames and smoke became a daunting task, made worse for my own peace of mind as I realized the fire was racing toward the homes of people I had known for decades, not to mention my own son's house.

When firefighters reported to me, they had uneasy looks on their faces. For many firefighters who had not been at 9/11, this was the biggest fire of their lives. All they could see were flames everywhere against the backdrop of darkness.

"Chief, it looks like the whole world is on fire!" one fire lieutenant told me. "What do you want us to do?"

I knew how they felt. It looked as if my own world was on fire. As I had done on 9/11, I had to narrow their focus to a specific mission. I gave one order: "Get me water!"

With Engine companies sitting in three feet of water, firefighters began drafting directly from flooded streets, stretching heavy hose through these storm-made lakes to relay pumpers and tower ladders—ordinary things but made extraordinarily difficult by driving rain and fierce fires.

However, the radiant heat and wind-driven convection currents were too hot and kept firefighters at bay; they could not make an initial, direct frontal attack. The fire roared with each gust of wind and breathed intense heat on buildings until the structures exploded into fifty-foot-high flames. Anything in its path was reduced to ashes.

Commanding at extreme events had taught me to visualize the incident as if I was standing on a hill or perched on a balcony overlooking the fire-ground. Having spent decades of summers in Breezy Point, I created a mental map of the blocks on fire. I generated command opportunities to battle this superstorm fire by anticipating fire movement and taking advantage of a wide break between one set of homes blocks away. This allowed me to position units for dynamic changes in fire behavior and wind direction.

My plan B was to get well ahead of the flames to cut off the fire's advance. I transmitted additional alarms with specific instructions for units to approach from the west and position apparatus three blocks ahead of the western fire front. Due to the scale of the fire and the unpredictable nature of hurricane winds, I had to think of the worst-case scenario. With a hundred homes burning, I made the difficult decision to give up dozens of homes to save hundreds.

FDNY firefighters, including a few off-duty members and Vollies, battled this unprecedented conflagration despite being cold and soaked to the bone. Suddenly, after six hours, the wind shifted from the southeast to out of the south. This allowed me to send the units I had prepositioned to stop the western advance of the fire.

By 7 a.m., the fire was contained. Exhausted, I passed command to my relief, who directed final extinguishment of smoldering rubble. As the sun began to rise, it became evident that a six-block stretch of homes had been destroyed by fire and others were severely damaged. It looked as if bombs had leveled a section of Breezy Point.

A paramedic on the scene observed the side of my face and said, "Chief, you should have that burn looked at by a doctor."

"Thanks, don't worry about me," I said. "It can't be that bad." I didn't even feel it. He then took a picture of the burn with his phone and showed it to me, reiterating, "Chief, this is a second-degree burn of your face that should be examined at the burn center."

One look at the picture and I knew he was right. I left with the paramedics.

At the New York Presbyterian Hospital's Burn Center on Manhattan's Upper East Side, the triage nurse examined me immediately upon seeing my white shirt black with soot and the burned side of my face. I explained to the doctor that the fire had been so fierce that no one could escape the shower of embers or the dense smoke—not even me, though I was a hundred yards away. I had to get back to work to make sure everyone was safe. The doctors and nursing staff attended to the burns, gave me some oxygen for taking in too much smoke, and then released me.

I called Ginny, working across the street at Memorial Sloan Kettering Cancer Center. She had been on duty since the previous day. I knew she was tired, and I could drive her home on my way back to Breezy Point.

"How about in an hour?" she said.

"Would it make a difference if I told you I was just discharged from the burn center?" I asked.

Ginny came running across the street. Over my career, I have scared her too many times. She gave me a big hug. (Thanks to the burn unit and Ginny's wound care, I have no scar.)

When I got back to Breezy Point, I learned that, after multiple searches, no bodies had been found and no one was reported missing—which was nothing short of miraculous. But the conflagration had totally destroyed 128 homes and severely damaged 22 others, making it the biggest residential fire in the FDNY's history. Our family's bungalow sustained substantial water damage to the first floor, and the heating and air-conditioning systems were destroyed, but we had been able to stop the fire less than two hundred feet away.

After the political leaders and the press left, I stood in the middle of the burned-out rubble. It felt like being on the Pile. Smoky mounds of debris stretched in all directions, but no one had died. Seeing my white helmet, residents started coming up to me. They had lost their homes. To my surprise, they thanked me for saving their community—my community—and all they wanted was a hug. Even when our whole world is on fire, we have each other.

EPILOGUE

O N EVERY ANNIVERSARY OF 9/11, I attend a memorial ceremony at the World Trade Center in my dress blue uniform. The names of all those killed on 9/11 and during the 1993 bombing are read aloud. For years, the anniversary commemorations were held at a dusty construction site until a memorial park was built with two reflective pools representing the footprints of the North and South Towers. Etched in stone around each pool are the names of those who died. The firefighters' names are grouped by their units, like Engine 33, a powerful symbol of how they responded to the attacks.

At each of the six significant moments, marking the crashing of four planes and the collapse of both World Trade Center towers, we pause as a fire bell rings five times, and that sequence repeats four times, 5-5-5-5. More than a thousand family members observe a minute of silence; those of us in uniform tender a slow, respectful salute, while close friends stand at our side covering their hearts. With each set of bells that echo across the memorial plaza, I replay in my mind what I was doing during those moments. I take the memories of my brother and my firefighters from deep within my heart to my conscious thoughts.

On 9/11, first responders demonstrated bravery from the very beginning. When seeing the towers burning, they asked in disbelief, "Wait . . . what?" Then, knowing the danger, they decided to enter, asking, "How can I help?" Their mission was to save those who were in their greatest moment of need. All of us, from firefighters to chiefs, shared the risk. These memories are as real on each anniversary as it was at the time. Those 102 minutes are my personal time with my heroes, who saved 20,000 people that day.

Many times, after the ceremony, I stop by my old Duane Street firehouse, often seeing Jules and some of the old guys.

When it became too taxing for my parents to go to the ceremony at the site, I would meet them and my sister at Engine 33, Ladder 9, my brother Kevin's old firehouse. The rigs are parked outside, and tables are set up on the apparatus floors. The 9/11 family members have a wonderful lunch with the firefighters, with lots of food and hugs to go around. Our ten families will always be part of this firehouse's family. It is like an extended family of cousins. You may not see them all the time, but when you do, it feels good. There is a metal plaque on the wall with the names of each firefighter lost. Their pictures also hang on a wall in the kitchen, so generations to come will never forget their faces.

In the evening, two beams of light representing the Twin Towers shine high into the night sky. It gives us a moment to pause and remember that day and how the world came together in sorrow and hope.

ON A CLEAR, crisp morning in 2014, the kind that December seems to give as a last gift before a cold winter, I walked into the lobby of the newly completed One World Trade Center. So pristine, so unlike the last time I had been in that spot—a different building on another bright morning when shattered glass covered the lobby and smoke billowed across the sky.

I thought of the old WTC with my firefighters, trying to rescue people from more than ninety countries. The resulting media attention gave all victims of terrorism a voice. We, the victims of terrorism, both international and domestic, join in supporting each other and speaking out about these terrible acts against humanity. In going through our trauma and waking up to sorrow, we are more aware of the kindness deep inside each other.

The new structure, which reaches 1,776 feet tall, is a symbol of hope for international cooperation to manage global challenges. It may also represent the simple kindness we can give to each other during these times.

My Port Authority hosts and I rode a high-speed elevator up to the observation deck. On a wall of the elevator, a large screen displayed the history of the WTC, its construction, the events of that day, and the years of rebuilding. While the observation deck was impressive, my hosts took me to a small, secured stair that led up to the roof. We went outside and climbed a narrow metal ladder, one step at a time, to get to a circular metal platform in the shadow of the 408-foot antenna spire. We were high above everything in New York City.

I breathed deeply as I took in the panorama before me. In every direction, another chapter of my life. Turning to the east, I saw the far side of the Brooklyn Bridge, a few blocks from FDNY headquarters, where, as a staff chief, I worked to change things. Farther into Brooklyn, I had spent my first six years in Crown Heights as a firefighter in Engine 234 and Ladder 123. Even from that distance, I could make out the spires of its many churches. Beyond that, I saw my old Queens neighborhoods, where my brother Kevin and I were raised and grew up to be firefighters.

Standing on top of the new skyscraper, built on the ashes of that day, I realized I had changed a lot since September 11, 2001. I value every day as extra and appreciate the people I care about, especially my wife, Ginny, children Christine and Gregory, and extending across almost a century, my mom, sister Mary Ellen, and grandchildren Emma and Maddie. I understand that any of this love can be suddenly snatched away.

I view the world differently. I no longer think of myself as just a New Yorker, but as being connected to all the people worldwide who run into difficult and dangerous situations. My world has expanded in ways I never imagined. It's bigger than the FDNY. I have traveled extensively across the U.S., Europe, and Asia and talked with others from every corner of the world about courage, leadership, and resilience in extraordinary times.

Extreme events from 9/11 to pandemics and natural disasters throw us into a global state of trauma. Worldwide, we collectively experience anxiety about the future and turn to crisis leaders to lessen this fear and uncertainty. For decades, I have studied crisis leadership and continue to teach about it in programs at the Harvard Kennedy School and Columbia University. I tell people how I made critical decisions when every moment counts and learned to lead with each disaster. But these stories are only as good as what I did with these experiences. I realized that without action there is no hope and without hope there is no leadership.

The heart of crisis leadership is the ability to sustain hope by unifying efforts to solve complex problems in the face of great tragedy. This often meant putting myself on the line to get diverse groups to work together. But by partnering with each other, we changed things so that we can depend on each other in a crisis.

It takes courage to find resilience, to come back to lead with greater determination and purpose. My journey started on 9/11, and it is what propelled me to make a difference over the years. But my most incredible privilege was sitting with other leaders and victims of terrorism and disasters from around the world. We shared stories, shed a few tears, and together turned traumatic memories into hope for the future.

As I looked down from on top of One World Trade Center to the streets below me, I took in Tribeca, Battery Park City, and lower Manhattan neighborhoods reborn from the ashes of 9/11. On Duane Street, I saw Engine 7, Ladder 1, and Battalion 1, my firehouse, where I was the closest chief to the Twin Towers. A little farther north was Kevin's company, Engine 33, in NoHo. That morning, units raced from firehouses all over the city to meet me in the North Tower's lobby to save as many lives as possible in 102 minutes.

Mike Hurley of the Port Authority, who had worked with me in the North Tower lobby so many years earlier, asked, "Chief, can you write something on the steel of the WTC?"

"Of course. It would be an honor," I said. He handed me a marker.

I took a moment to think. What could I leave for generations to come? I felt small standing on top of this famous skyscraper representing a defining moment in history and hope for the future. I focused on two questions many people asked me after 9/11.

The first question is, "How do you define a hero?"

I initially sensed an answer that morning in the burning towers. For me, "a hero is one who does ordinary things in extraordinary times." I saw that on 9/11, when firefighters running up told people coming down the stairs, "Don't stop. You can make it out of here. Keep going." Survivors have since told me, "It meant so much having firefighters tell us to keep going, and we did, and we made it out." In extraordinary times in history, people do ordinary things when it counts the most.

The second question was much harder. It was the hardest question I was ever asked in my career and perhaps in my life, a question that every chief or commander dreads to hear from family members and friends of responders lost in disasters. In the aftermath of 9/11, I heard it from so many people, including my own family: "Why did my loved one have to run into the burning towers?"

My thoughts went back to July 9, 2005. The day my family dedicated a statue of Saint Florian, patron saint of firefighters, at St. John Cemetery in Queens, where my brother is buried in a family plot. Since many 9/11 firefighters are buried there, my parents wanted the statue to represent all firefighters and first responders who died running into the towers.

During the small ceremony, some friends and the local fire companies stood with my family and me as I read the dedication inscription. My teenage son Greg played "Amazing Grace" on the bagpipes. In my short talk, I tried to answer this question that people had asked me for years, often with tears in their eyes.

It was not enough to say that it was our job. My parents and families of first responders deserved more. Their question lingered with me for a long time until I realized the answer was always there right in front of us.

On a beautiful sunny day that reminded me of that terrible Tuesday morning, I said, "We ran into the burning towers on 9/11, so others may live. And today, we first responders continue to run into danger for others."

My family and my firefighters looked at me as if to say, *Of course*. The answer was always there, but it just took time to work through the pain so we could see it.

From unthinkable tragedy and deep reflection, I came to realize that the courage of ordinary heroes is in each one of us. We have the power to make a difference by doing ordinary things in life's most challenging times. Each of us, sooner or later, will be presented with a moment to be an ordinary hero.

Now I knew what I had to write on the steel at the top of One World Trade Center. I took out my marker and wrote:

> *Always remember the heroes,*
> *who did ordinary things,*
> *at extraordinary times,*
> *so others may live.*

And I signed it, Chief Joseph Pfeifer.

ACKNOWLEDGMENTS

Even twenty years after, this story was not an easy one for me to tell. I had to search my memory of an unthinkable day, and all that followed, recalling so many critical moments and countless faces. The stress of putting words on paper intensified the experience, but in a good way, prompting me to connect and reconnect with many people without whom I could not have written this memoir.

The journey toward this book started with me wanting to write an academic book on crisis leadership. My marvelous literary agent, Lisa Queen, encouraged me instead first to tell my personal story. She immediately got Portfolio/Penguin Random House on board. The team led by Adrian Zackheim and guided by Bria Sandford with the assistance of Nina Rodríguez-Marty became trusted partners who provided support and urged me to keep going.

I could not have crafted this book without the wonderful assistance of Glenna Whitley, who cared about every story and was always willing to get on long phone calls to discuss how to shape each chapter. Thanks to Kate

Frucher, Tim Herlocker, and Arn Howitt, who each in their own way helped me with the book drafts by providing valuable feedback and encouragement. I am incredibly grateful to Jules and Gédéon Naudet, who shared their film, transcripts, and interview recollections with me, catapulting me back in time. Jules especially taught me how to tell my story in scenes and characters.

I could not be more appreciative of Gary Marlon Suson, Jean Nichols, and Jeff Kowalsky, who provided me with very personal pictures. Screenshots from the Naudet 9/11 documentary gave us a valuable glimpse inside the North Tower.

I'm grateful to my mentors, colleagues, and all the firefighters I worked with in my thirty-seven years in the FDNY. From the firehouse where I was a probie to headquarters where I was an assistant chief. A special thanks to all who were part of the Duane Street firehouse, where we shared stories of bravery about that day and our journey to resilience. Thanks to Fire Commissioner Sal Cassano, Chief of Department Pete Hayden, Assistant Chief Joe Callan, and many others whom I worked closely with that day and for many years to follow. I appreciate all those dedicated people who worked with me at FDNY's Center for Terrorism and Disaster Preparedness to connect agencies for collaboration and coordination. It was an honor to serve New York City and the FDNY with all of you. This was especially true on 9/11 and the period after, where we needed to support each other to imagine better ways of doing things.

I am also thankful to have worked with Lieutenant Colonel Reid Sawyer, Professor Nelly Lahoud, and so many others from the Combating Terrorism Center at West Point.

Many thanks to all those who took my classes on crisis leadership at the FDNY, the U.S. Military Academy, the Harvard Kennedy School, the Naval Postgraduate School, Columbia University, and Tsinghua University. Your questions got me to think more deeply about what I have learned from my experiences.

ACKNOWLEDGMENTS

I appreciate the talks I had with Chief James Schwartz of the Arlington Fire Department and Special Agent in Charge Christopher Combs of the FBI, who demonstrated unified operations at the Pentagon on 9/11. Exchanging ideas with my 9/11 colleagues at the Harvard Kennedy School enabled each of us to imagine better when encountering extreme events.

I owe a lot to my outstanding Harvard Kennedy School colleagues, Professors Arn Howitt and Dutch Leonard. For more than fifteen years, we have taught at Harvard and around the world about leading in a crisis. This guided us to conduct international research on responding to novel and extreme events.

My Harvard friends and I, with Jules Naudet, traveled to Paris, France, to conduct research after the November 13, 2015, attacks on Paris and then again after the fire at the Cathedral of Notre Dame in 2019. We talked to everyone, from the prime minister and mayor of Paris to generals and firefighters of the Paris Fire Brigade, from SWAT officers and commissioner with the Research and Intervention Brigade (BRI) to hostages taken in the Bataclan, as well as doctors who cared for victims. We saw our personal experiences in each other's stories, which the Naudet brothers portray in their films. Perhaps it was through the eyes of others that I learned how to write my 9/11 story.

For all our work with first responders in Paris, I was given several unique privileges. The first was standing in the seventeenth-century courtyard of Les Invalides, being made an honorary firefighter of the Paris Fire Brigade. The second was receiving the high honor of being installed as Chevalier of the Ordre National du Mérite by decree of the president of France.

And as a display of global friendship and bravery, I got to scale the outer steel structure of the Eiffel Tower with the BRI and Jules. Attached by a rope to one BRI officer above me and one below me, I firmly placed one foot at a time on each cross section of steel as I climbed the iconic structure. Then I got to use my firefighting training and rappelled down, seeing the beautiful city of Paris like few have ever done. That moment was key to my understanding of how international friendship and cooperation shape our response to difficult challenges.

My biggest thank-you goes to my wife, Ginny. I could not have written this book or gotten through these events without your love and support. You are always my hero. A very special appreciation to our daughter, Christine, and her daughter, our first granddaughter, Emma; our son, Gregory, his wife, Cristina, and their daughter, our second granddaughter, Maddie; my sister, Mary Ellen, her husband, Victor, and family. And I cannot forget my ninety-five-year-old mom, Helen: you make everything so wonderful with your smiles and unconditional love.

Finally, thanks to all the ordinary heroes who marked an extraordinary time in history by doing ordinary things for others. I will carry you always in my heart.

BIBLIOGRAPHY

Corrigan, M., P. Greene, D. Kane, G. Christ, and S. Lynch. *FDNY Crisis Counseling*. Hoboken, NJ: John Wiley & Sons, Inc., 2006.

Dwyer, J., and K. Flynn. *102 Minutes: The Untold Story of the Fight to Survive inside the Twin Towers*. New York: Times Books, 2005.

McGonigal, Kelly. *The Upside of Stress*. New York: Avery, 2015.

McKinsey & Company. *Increasing FDNY's Preparedness*. New York: New York City Fire Department, 2002.

National Commission on Terrorist Attacks upon the United States. *The 9/11 Commission Report*: *Final Report of the National Commission on Terrorist Attacks upon the United States*. New York: W. W. Norton, 2004.

National Institute of Standards and Technology. *Federal Building and Fire Safety Investigation of the World Trade Center Disaster: Emergency Response Operations*. Gaithersburg, MD: NIST, December 1, 2005.

———. *Federal Building and Fire Safety Investigation of the World Trade Center Disaster: Final Report on the Collapse of World Trade Center 7*. Gaithersburg, MD: NIST, 2008.

Naudet, Gédéon, and Jules Naudet. *9/11: The Filmmakers' Commemorative Edition* [film]. Paramount, 2002.

Pfeifer, J. "Hurricane Sandy Sparks a Conflagration in Breezy Point." *WNYF* Magazine 13, no. 2 (2013): 24–28.

———. "Understanding How Organizational Bias Influenced First Responders at the World Trade Center." In B. Bongar et al., eds. *Psychology of Terrorism*. New York: Oxford University Press, 2007.

———, and J. Merlo. "The Decisive Moment: The Science of Decision Making Under Stress." In P. Sweeney, M. Matthew, and P. Lester, eds. *Leadership in Dangerous*

Situations: A Handbook for the Armed Forces, Emergency Services, and First Responders. Annapolis: Naval Institute Press, 2011.

"The Sept. 11 Records." *New York Times,* archive.nytimes.com/www.nytimes.com /packages/html/nyregion/20050812_WTC_GRAPHIC/met_WTC_histories_full_01 .html.

Smith, D. *Report from Ground Zero.* New York: Viking, 2002.

Sutherland, Audrey. *Paddling My Own Canoe.* Honolulu: University Press of Hawaii, 1978.